MW01094078

You Can
UNDERSTAND
the Book *of*
REVELATION

A CLEAR GUIDE TO INTERPRETING PROPHECY

JEFF SCOGGINS

Copyright © 2013 by
Jeff Scoggins

For more resources from Jeff Scoggins visit www.scoggins.biz.

Scripture quotations are taken from the New International Version unless
otherwise marked. The HOLY BIBLE, NEW INTERNATIONAL VER-
SION®. Copyright © 1973, 1978, 1984 Biblica. Used by permission of
Zondervan. All rights reserved.

Scripture quotations marked KJV are taken from the King James Version
of the Bible.

Scripture quotations marked NKJV are taken from the New King James
Version®. Copyright © 1982 by Thomas Nelson, Inc. Used by permission.
All rights reserved.

Edited by Tim Lale.

Printed in the United States of America. All rights reserved.

ISBN 978-0-9889914-0-8

Contents

Getting Started

I attended my first prophecy series in Tennessee when I was about seven years old. I have been a part of many since then, trying to expand my knowledge and understanding. In spite of my interest and study, however, prophecy interpretation simply wouldn't stick in my mind. I filled my Bible margins with dates, charts, and interpretations, only to find that the next time I visited a passage, everything was mixed up in my mind again. I couldn't recall what particular symbols represented and how they fit together. To make matters worse, presenters often disagreed with each other, confusing me all the more.

It wasn't until I took Professor Jon Paulien's seminary class in the exegesis[1] of Revelation that prophecy finally fell into place for me. Before that class, I thought I knew some basics of interpreting prophecy. Turns out I didn't. I was surprised at how much was new material for me—an entirely different way to approach prophecy than I had encountered before.

Dr. Paulien's class changed my life as a person and as a pastor. Suddenly Revelation had a storyline, a plot I could follow that held everything together. And the gospel of Jesus Christ finally shone through the clutter of symbols, interpretations, and sensationalism that had always shrouded the prophecies for me.

After the class was over, I took a portion of the material I had learned and, with Dr. Paulien's blessing, turned it into a seminar. Now it appears in this book. I cannot take credit for most of the content we will be studying because it closely follows Dr. Paulien's class. That said, however, this is my own approach to the material. Although much of the wording comes directly from the class, not all of it does. Dr. Paulien would surely add, delete, and state many concepts differently than I have. I thank him for his generosity and urge you to read his books for a deeper understanding of this complex subject. I particularly recommend *The Deep Things of God* and

---

1. *Exegesis*, a simplified definition: The process of interpreting a biblical passage while taking into account the original context, language, and intent of the author. *Exegesis* draws meaning out of the text, in contrast to *eisegesis*, which reads meaning into it.

Armageddon at the Door, from Review and Herald Publishing Association.

A word about the structure of the book

This book is divided into two sections. The first seven chapters are largely about method, attempting to lay out in practical terms the way we should go about interpreting prophecy using only the Bible.

The second section uses these principles to examine the "plot" of Armageddon—both the plot against God's faithful people by the forces of evil and also the plot (the storyline) that runs through the central portion of the book of Revelation.

Although Armageddon sounds terrible, the fact remains that Jesus is the central figure throughout. The climax of the great controversy between Christ and Satan will be an incredible time in the history of the universe. It's time we stop viewing the final events of Bible prophecy in the shadow of fear and begin viewing them in the light of the hope we have in Jesus. He is the story of Revelation from beginning to end.

Section 1
How to Decipher the Symbols

Chapter 1

The Process

Several years ago I built my own workshop. When I had finished, I stood back and studied what I had done and felt pleased with my work. That moment of satisfaction had been a long time in coming, because I had built the shop in one-hour increments over many days, slipping in that one hour a day between my pastoral work and time spent with my wife and one-year-old child. So, most of the time during its construction, my shop was just a skeleton. Still, I enjoyed watching the building go up. I could see progress, slow though it was.

Before I began building the skeleton of my project, I had to dig the foundation, which I did with a shovel. I have to admit that it was tedious. However, I understood that if I didn't construct the foundation well, I would regret it later.

We must go through the same building process in learning to interpret prophecy. Naturally we will look forward to the end, when we can step back and look at the incredible picture we've constructed from the book of Revelation. And we know that we must spend time building our case in order to arrive at a good end product. First we have to build a solid foundation of safe Bible study and interpretation.

I've discovered over the years that some people find building this foundation a little tedious if they simply want to know the meaning of the mark of the beast. But we will discover some disturbing things in prophecy, things that may cause us to rethink some of our preconceptions. Therefore, we need to know that we're standing on a solid foundation of biblical truth.

In the course of this study, we'll not attempt to identify every character and symbol we encounter in the book of Revelation, because our primary focus is the plot of the book and how Jesus Christ inhabits every corner of it. If for now we skip trying to identify and explain every last symbol, a storyline will emerge with greater clarity. After that, we will be able to plug in the identities of the different characters and everything will fall into place. We can't avoid identifying some of the characters as we go along, but that's not our primary goal.

I've broken down the entire study into three stages. Here is a preview of where we're heading.

Stage One: Foundation

First, we're going to lay a foundation by

- Looking at why we are interested in this topic at all
- Looking at Revelation in the light of the author's time in history
- Considering our limitations
- Discussing safe methods of approaching the Bible, and prophecy in particular
- Looking at how the gospel figures into Revelation
- Seeing how the prologue of Revelation gives us some checks and balances for our interpretations.

Stage Two: Building the skeleton

Next we will dive into the text of Revelation itself and start making sense out of it using the tools we gained in Stage One. Our study will take a distinct shift when we start building a big picture of the events taking place at the end of this world's history.

In these chapters we will see

- Three stages of Christian history and the stage we are living in
- How the forces of evil battle the forces of good in a great end-time conflict
- Who are God's and Satan's forces
- What those forces will look like and what they will be doing and saying
- The nature of their battle.

Among the characters and symbols we will encounter in this second stage will be

- Dragons
- Women
- Beasts
- God's end-time people
- Armageddon
- The mark of the beast
- And much more.

Stage Three: The final product

Finally, at the end we will step back from the details in which we've been immersed and we'll see the big picture. We will see the plot of Revelation, and we'll actually be able to chart the sequence of events surrounding the end of time leading up to Jesus' second coming. We will also be able to see quite specifically where we now stand in time.

By the time we get there, we will be able to take some pride in what we have accomplished because of the careful foundational work we will have done along the way. We will have arrived at some startling conclusions, but we'll have carefully marked and studied our way there, so we can have a healthy measure of confidence that we've arrived at the proper place.

Everything we do will be grounded in the Bible text. It's tempting to jump over to history and find scenarios that seem to confirm the prophecies, and there is a time and place for that kind of examination, but it's not here and now. We're going to limit ourselves to only the Bible for this study.

Study Guide Outline

Chapter 1

1. In Stage One we will lay a _____ for seeing the underlying story of Revelation.

2. In Stage Two we will use our particular _____ of Bible study to begin making sense of the text.

3. In Stage Three we will paint the big picture and see a flow chart of the _____ of events at the end of the world.

Chapter 2

It's About the Story

The journey of interpreting prophecy takes us on a trap-laden trail. Being aware of the traps helps us to avoid them.

The first trap we will avoid is attempting to interpret prophecy in bits and pieces without consulting the rest of the Bible or without consulting the immediate context of the passage we're trying to interpret.

Let's say I took my squealing car to a mechanic and the way he addressed my problem was to announce, "A squeal means a faulty belt." That might sound good except that I know the sound is coming from the rear of the vehicle, not the engine. "Sorry," he says, "that's impossible. We have figured this out, and a squeal is undoubtedly caused by the serpentine belt." And he won't budge from his opinion.

I will go to another mechanic who doesn't claim to have my engine noise figured out without checking properly. A good mechanic listens to the squeal of my car and suspects something, but if his first guess is wrong, he knows something else to check. How does he have any clue what else to look for? Because he understands the "story" of an automobile. He understands the principles upon which a car works, and therefore he has the ability to track down a car's problems. A careful mechanic is ever growing in his knowledge and experience with vehicles, so that the longer he works with them, the better he works on them.

We often approach the Bible and prophecy in the same way as the first mechanic. We have decided that a symbol means just one thing and no discussion is possible. But we are much better served when we approach prophecy as the second mechanic does—when we discover the underlying story. When we do that, we are forced to admit that not every symbol is perfectly clear at the outset.

That's the first trap to avoid. Don't try to interpret prophecy without putting in the work of testing interpretations by the rest of the Bible. That means we need a sound method of studying the Bible that produces accurate conclusions.

The Bible interprets its own symbols

Another trap to avoid is attempting to interpret prophecy by using sources from outside of the Bible.

Many people "study" prophecy by watching preachers on television. One of the first things some of my Bible students want to know when I teach a prophecy class is whether I am familiar with television preacher so-and-so, and they give me a name. Usually I've never heard of the person. They sometimes believe that a particular preacher has all the answers.

Others study prophecy using commentaries and books on the subject. If you happen upon a commentary or book by a scholar who is on the right track, you are fortunate, but how do you know who is on the right track? The only way is to crack open your own Bible and learn it for yourself.

The more time we spend searching the Scriptures, the more able we are to figure out the true meaning of the symbols. The Bible has the keys to itself. It will unlock its own mysterious symbols to anyone who will approach it in a systematic way, like a sleuth tracking down the clues that lead to the solution. Yes, it is work, but it is also the most rewarding work you can do. The brain exercise is priceless.

The Holy Spirit has an active role in our study because, as the Bible says, "Spiritual things are spiritually discerned." If you don't spend daily time with God to know Him better by reading His word and praying, then you won't get far with trying to interpret prophecy. If you resolve to know Jesus as your Lord and friend, then in that relationship you will have a source of guidance for searching prophecy because you will be open to the Holy Spirit speaking to you in your study.

Avoid the tempting trap of "studying" prophecy without opening your Bible or only opening it at the places suggested by someone else. Know the Bible for yourself.

Prophecy is fuzzy

Another trap to avoid is trying to become the next Nostradamus, attempting to predict the future using Bible prophecy.

Prophecy by its very nature is not an exact science. God never intended for prophecy to fill in every single detail about the future. At best, to use Paul's phrase, we are "looking through a glass darkly." From prophecy we get a general idea about the future, but it's only a general idea—not the detailed description that we might sometimes wish for.

I fear that history is repeating itself. A couple of thousand years ago, some Israelites thought they had the prophecies concerning the Messiah all figured out. I've read about their interpretations of those prophecies, and I admit they were convincing. I would have believed them at that time. By their interpretations they were convinced they knew how the Messiah would conquer Rome and make Israel the leading power on earth. Those Israelites either ignored or failed to recognize the parts of the prophecies that went contrary to their preconceived ideas, and therefore their eyes were closed to key parts of the whole picture. So when the prophecies were actually fulfilled, it turned out that their interpretations were wrong.

I fear that today we have become so attached to the particular details of the way we understand prophecy that we may be blinded to other possibilities. We need to come to terms with the fact that looking into the future is never going to be as clear as we might imagine it. Prophecy only becomes crystal clear in hindsight.

The primary purpose of prophecy is not to satisfy our curiosity about the future but to show us how to live today. We must become students of prophecy in such a way that, whatever form the fulfillment of prophecy takes, we'll be positioned to recognize it for what it is.

So don't try to be Nostradamus and predict the future by using Bible prophecy. Accept the fact that looking into the future is not clear.

Study Guide Outline

Chapter 2

1. We need a sound _____ of interpreting prophecy.

2. The Bible _____ its own symbols.

3. Prophecy is clear in _____ but fuzzy when it points to the future.

Chapter 3

About Revelation

Most people believe that the same John who wrote the Gospel of John and 1, 2, and 3 John is also the author of the book of Revelation. However, some contention has arisen over this assertion, because those proficient in ancient Greek have seen that the grammar of the Gospel of John and 1, 2, and 3 John is good Greek grammar, while the grammar of Revelation is not good—about the equivalent of fifth-grade Greek. So how could someone who wrote so well in other books be the same person who wrote so badly in Revelation? It's a fair question, and one that has a good answer.

The book of Revelation was probably written around AD 95, when John was exiled on the island of Patmos. There, John would not have had access to a luxury he had earlier, when he wrote his other books of the Bible: the luxury of an editor. For his other books he would have had scribes around who could correct his Greek, just as, when I lived in Russia, I had a secretary who could correct my lousy Russian. Letters came out of my office in perfect Russian, bearing my signature. If I had been forced to write my own letters, the results would have been less than pretty.

So in a way the bad grammar of Revelation can serve to confirm that John wrote the book. Greek was the working language of the world in John's day, just as English is the working language of our world today. Every Hebrew boy studied Greek to about the fifth grade. Thus, without editorial assistance John wrote Greek at the proficiency of a fifth grader.

Authority

Understanding the differences in the grammar of John's various books helps us avoid the trap of believing that the Bible is verbally inspired, as though God had written it with his own finger.

Verbal inspiration is the trap of believing that God dictated every particular word of the Bible and that the human being who wielded the pen really had nothing to do with what came out of the pen. In this belief, the writer was remotely controlled from heaven.

If that is true then God writes with bad grammar some of the time. It makes more sense that God inspired John's heart and mind, but John still wrote what he saw in his own words with Holy Spirit guidance. If God had written the Bible with his own finger, as he did the Ten Commandments, he may well have used different words than the Bible writers actually did. But for some reason God has chosen to limit himself and work through fallible human beings.

However, this does not mean that the Bible will ever steer us wrong. It will not. Contained in the Bible is everything we need for salvation. An illustration may help. When you buy the latest electronic gadget, a manual usually comes with it. Sometimes that manual is written is terrible English, but it works anyway. Once we get past the poor grammar, we soon have our gadget working correctly. The manual guided us flawlessly to the goal it was intended for, even though the guide itself wasn't flawless.

Bad grammar or inconsistencies in the text of the Bible should not make us think the Bible is disqualified as the word of God. It only reminds us that God is working with imperfect tools, as amazing as that may seem. The Bible isn't technically flawless, but *it is perfect for what it is designed for.*

That said, though, the idea of technical imperfections has the potential to call into question the authority of the Bible. So we should discuss briefly some issues of authority and how we relate to the idea that God works through imperfect humans.

Ultimate authority exists only in God himself, and the Bible, though it comes from God, is not God himself. Thus the Bible is a different level of authority, one that we could call biblical authority. This biblical level of authority is God speaking through his prophets. By tossing in the variable of human prophets as authors, we must assume some limitations.

1. Accommodation

First of all, the Bible must accommodate the human situation. Since the prophet is writing within his time in history and in his language and culture, we must recognize that our understanding as we read depends a lot on understanding the prophet's time and context.

When we read Shakespeare, we have a different language experience than when we read a modern author. In order to understand Shakespeare, we must invest some time in understanding Elizabethan English and what life was like during Shakespeare's time—back in the time of "thee" and "thou" in England. If we don't do that, his plays won't make much sense.

We are limited in our understanding of the Bible because we don't live during the time that the prophet lived. In reading the Bible we must realize that God was speaking to John on John's turf and allow that to affect our understanding.

2.   The Bible doesn't answer every question explicitly

The second thing to note is that the Bible doesn't explicitly deal with every question we have. The Bible does not address eating donuts, for instance, because donuts didn't exist back then. But do you think that God has an opinion on whether or not you should eat a dozen donuts all in one sitting? Your mother would have an opinion, and, of course, God does too. But he does not speak to donuts directly.

We must assume that a God who is living and active in the world today must have an opinion on everything that is going on in our world. So, even though the Bible does not address every question explicitly, it does provide principles that will guide us in all our questions. If we systematically learn from God's word, we glean principles that give us a good idea of where God stands in pretty much every situation.

3.   The Bible is mostly stories

Even though we may use the Bible systematically to answer questions, the Bible is not written as systematic theology. You don't find lists of beliefs in the Bible or lists of answers to questions. The Bible is mostly stories. We draw lessons from those stories on how God would have us live today. And to many people's chagrin, this leaves open a wide arena of interpretation, which is another limitation in biblical authority that we must accept.

4.   Interpretive temptations

Finally, we must address our tendency to misread the Bible to suit our own purposes. It's too easy to approach the Bible with the intent of defending what we already believe rather than coming into it with an attitude of pure learning. Sometimes we have more confidence in what we think we know of the Bible than we should have. When it comes to interpreting the Bible, we need a good measure of self-distrust. That reminds us of another trap to avoid.

Ladder of Humility

Another trap we must avoid is over-confidence in our interpretations of prophecy. Consider what has been called the ladder of humility:

1. The first rung on the ladder of humility is what you know. You may not be the smartest person in the world, but you may have been educated in good schools, perhaps traveled the world, can fix a lot of different things with your hands, or do calculus or build electronics. You might feel as though you know quite a bit. However, the next rung on the ladder is far beyond anything you or anyone else on earth could ever reach.

2. The next rung on the ladder is everything that everyone on earth knows. If we lump all of that knowledge together, it's a formidable amount of knowledge. There's no chance of you or me ever mastering it all. However, the next rung on the ladder is far beyond this one.

3. The third rung on the ladder is what everyone on this earth could know if they had an infinite amount of time and resources. My mind is already boggled. And yet this rung also is nothing compared to the next one.

4. The next rung on the ladder is everything that every created being in the universe knows. If we consider the angels and the inhabitants of other created planets, the kind of knowledge and intelligence at that level is beyond anything we can understand. And yet this rung of the ladder of humility is still nothing compared to the next.

5. The final rung is what God knows.

With that perspective, what do we as individuals know? Very, very little!

Another concept we must understand as we delve into prophecy is that God meets us where we are, as extremely limited human beings. God does not require us to rise to his level in order to understand what he tells us. We are incapable of doing that. He comes down to our level, just as we do with our children. We don't explain in college-level language what we want a two-year-old to understand.

God speaks to his prophets in their own language and time

Even inspired writers like John knew very little. Knowing this helps us avoid another trap, thinking that in prophecy God is speaking only to us in our time right now.

We must understand that in prophecy God speaks to his prophets in their own language and time using their history as his point of reference. In other words, if you were a prophet right now, God would speak to you in the twenty-first-century version of your language, not ancient Hebrew or Greek or Aramaic. Why? Because you wouldn't understand him in those languages.

He would also speak to you in your cultural context, which involves things like airplanes, cars, computers, and so on. He wouldn't speak to you as if you lived in a historical context of spears and swords and chariots, and he wouldn't speak to you in a futuristic context of laser blasters and space vacations. Why not? Because you wouldn't understand him.

God is able to tell his stories in ways that make sense to each person. Think of Daniel 2 and Daniel 7 as an illustration. God sent the same message to two different people in two different ways. To the pagan king Nebuchadnezzar God sent a vision of an idol, because this is what a pagan would understand. To the Hebrew prophet Daniel he spoke with a vision of animals that was more in line with the story of Creation. The visions had the same message, but they employed different symbols to reach the receiver in his context.

God speaks the language of the person he is talking to using symbols which that person will understand. Yet, even though God voluntarily limits himself by coming down to a human level and speaking in the ancient prophet's language and context, this does not mean his intentions are lost for future generations. God makes sure that his ultimate goals will be accomplished even though he spoke in a particular language at a certain point in human history.

God speaks to his prophets using words from their upbringing and history, and we must accept that he used John's context in Revelation, not ours. Therefore, to truly understand Revelation, we must take John's time and culture into account. To understand prophecy we must learn to interpret prophecy through the prophet's eyes as much as we can, because this is bound to affect our interpretation today.

God's intent through human intent

On the other hand, we don't want to fall into the trap of thinking that since God was speaking to John in AD 95, there's no need to study the prophecy today. Just because God spoke in John's context does not mean that what was written two thousand years ago has no application for us in the twenty-first century, nor does it mean that it has application only to the twenty-first century and not for AD 95. We will see that it can apply to both.

Like all Bible prophets, John had his own goal in writing Revelation. He was concerned about the fate of the new churches that he and the other apostles had started. He had been praying for them, and Jesus appeared to him on Patmos in response to those prayers. Jesus instructed John to write a letter to those churches, describing his vision of the present and the future. That was John's goal in writing Revelation: to reach out and encourage and teach those in the seven new churches. And of course, the book of Revelation accomplished that goal.

How much John understood the significance his writing would have for the end of time, we cannot know, but through John's goal of encouraging the churches, God achieved his goal of giving his church throughout the ages a prophecy about the end of time. So even though John had his own intent for Revelation, God had a larger intent for the book, whether John realized it or not.

We see this kind of double achievement in many Bible prophecies. We call them dual prophecies. Take for instance, Jesus' prophecy in the book of Mark: "When you see the abomination of desolation standing where it ought not be standing, flee to the mountains" (Mark 13:14, paraphrased). Virtually all scholars agree that this prophecy applied to those living in Jerusalem in AD 70 as well as to the end of time. However, God intended more application for that prophecy than people realized in AD 70.

Dual application is a common function of prophecy. John probably didn't understand all of the implications of what he wrote for the future, but he did understand the implications for his own day and some of the ones for the future.

Let the Bible writers speak for themselves

Another trap we must avoid is reading the Bible as though it says what we want it to say. We must let the Bible writers speak for themselves.

Jeremiah 17:9 says, "The heart is deceitful above all things." We are prone to self-deception. Consequently we are tempted to read the Bible in a way that confirms what we already believe. That is a dangerous *hermeneutic*, or theory of Bible study. It is dangerous to study the Bible only to defend our preconceived ideas. We don't usually think of Bible reading as dangerous, but it can be. We must read the Bible safely. We must learn a hermeneutic, a method of Bible study, that allows the Bible to speak to us rather than us making it say what we want it to say.

The safe way to approach the Bible

1. Approach Bible study with prayer and a great deal of self-distrust, and with the humbling knowledge of how limited we are and how powerful and wise God is. Bible study isn't merely an academic exercise; it's life changing.

2. Another way to approach the Bible more safely is not to assume that any particular Bible translation[2] is perfect. Every translation has its biases, and none is perfect. It would be ideal for us to read the Scriptures in the original languages, but most of us don't have that ability. So the next best thing is to consult a variety of translations to clarify God's intended meaning.

3. If we read a text in five different translations and the wording of the text is the same in all of them, we know the original text was clear. If the text is different in all of them, we know the original was unclear and the translators didn't agree. If four versions are the same and one is different, we can suspect that a bias probably came through. The original was probably pretty clear but someone disagreed anyway, based on a personal view.

4. Another way to read your Bible safely is to give clear texts the priority over unclear ones, because in clear texts we have solid footing. In the unclear texts we can come up with about anything we want. The clear texts protect us from going wrong with the unclear texts.

5. Another way to read your Bible safely is to give general reading a higher priority than intensive studying. This might sound strange, but think about it: when we study the Bible we can control our perception of it by joining texts together from different books or chapters. It's easy in that situation to make the Bible say whatever we want. However, when we simply read it through and understand it, the text itself is in control of our perception, as it should be.

---

2. Don't confuse a translation with a paraphrase. A paraphrase is usually written by one person who's giving his or her personal take on the Bible, such as in *The Message* or *The Clear Word*. A translation is produced by scholars using the oldest version of the original languages available. Everything from the King James Version to the New International Version fits in this category.

6. That's not to say there's no place for study; there certainly is. But we should give most of our time to general reading as a precaution against our own biases. We all have them, and we can't get away from them entirely. There is safety in knowing what's in all of the Bible, not just the parts we choose to study.

7. Finally, you are safer studying the Bible if you don't always study alone. We need to study with others as well. The fact that someone might disagree with us and stir our thinking is a positive thing. They can teach us more than those we agree with because we then must defend what we believe.

Study Guide Outline

Chapter 3

1. The reason the book of Revelation has bad _____ is that on Patmos, John had no access to an editor.

2. Five limitations of biblical authority are:

   a. _____ to the human situation

   b. The Bible doesn't answer every _____

   c. Bible stories that are open to varieties of _____

   d. The temptation to try to make the Bible defend what we already _____

   e. We should approach the Bible with a great deal of _____ because we are limited in our understanding.

3. God speaks to his prophets in their own _____ and time in ways the prophet will understand.

4. God _____ himself by coming down to our level.

5. God's _____ for prophecy comes through even if the prophet doesn't understand that part of it.

6. Safe ways to approach the Bible:

   a. Come with _____ and self-distrust

   b. Use _____ translations

   c. Give _____ texts the priority

   d. Give general _____ higher priority than study

   e. Study with _____

Chapter 4

Basic Method for Interpreting Revelation

Two men were building houses. One man was patient and willing to take longer on his house. The other man was impatient and wanted his house to be finished ASAP. They lived in a hurricane-prone area near the ocean, so the first man selected an area of solid rock for his building spot. In order to build his foundation, he went at the rock with a jackhammer and a sledgehammer and maybe even a little bit of well-placed dynamite. His progress was excruciatingly slow. But he was patient.

The other man decided he was interested in the view he could get for his house by building close to the water. When he saw how slow the first guy was going, well, he wasn't patient enough to go to all that work of digging deep. He wet down some sand so that it would pack really well and started building his subfloor right on top of the sand, which when wet seemed stable enough. Once he had the subfloor done, he put up walls and trusses and slapped plywood over everything. He was finishing with drywall by the time the first man had completed his foundation.

The second man was done with building his house in no time flat. He moved his family in, and they barbecue on the balcony while the first man was still carefully building his house. Eventually the first man finished as well. On the surface, the houses looked pretty similar. The one nearer the ocean arguably had a better view.

October arrived and, along with it, hurricane season. The first hurricane was barely a hurricane, but it brought rain that poured down on the houses. The streams running into the ocean swelled and overran their banks. The wind lashed the houses. And the house built on sand fell with a great crash, while the house that had rock for its foundation stood firm.

You recognize the paraphrased story from the book of Matthew. Jesus told it in his famous sermon on the mount—minus the jackhammers and dynamite.

One of the primary ways we can build a solid foundation for the work we will be doing in Revelation is to give serious thought to how we'll go about interpreting the book. If we approach prophecy impatiently and hurriedly, we may very well build ourselves a house on the sand that will not withstand the hurricane of scrutiny and truth. If we take time to be sure that we are using safe methods for interpreting prophecy, we're going to be able to stand on much stronger truth.

Safe method for interpreting prophecy
1. Read lightly and broadly.

When approaching the book of Revelation, first read the passage lightly and broadly. That means taking it all in but not stopping along the way. Reading narrowly and stopping to pick at things without the overall context in mind will not help us in interpreting the prophecies. Don't read only the part you are interested in, but read around it also. Simply get a feel for the whole passage and some of the surrounding context. It's good to read it over a few times.

2. Read intensively.

Next, follow your light reading with intensive reading. Look for and define key words—the words that really make a difference. Make sure you understand those words. Look them up in the original Greek. You don't have to know the language to do that. Computers and the Internet make it easy, and there are also books that help you do it.[3]

3. Compare translations.

Next, compare the passage as it is given in several translations of the Bible.[4] Note whether the translation is similar in each case or which ones differ significantly, not only in wording but also in shades of meaning. Think about what the differences tell you.

4. Consider word relationships.

Now look at word relationships. Words have different meanings based on the words around them. For instance, the word *inhabitant* might just be a word to describe someone who lives in a particular place. But

---

3. For example, *A Greek - English Lexicon of the New Testament and other Early Christian Literature* or the popular *Greek Strong's Dictionary of the New Testament.*
4. A number of Bible websites help with this:
    Biblegateway.com, Biblestudytools.com, and e-sword.net.

when we put the words "inhabitants of the earth" together, we find that John uses that phrase quite often and with particular significance in Revelation. It's something important for us to recognize.

5. Consider Old Testament background.

Pay careful attention to the Old Testament background in connection with the passage. The footnotes in many Bibles will point out these connections. We're going to look into this in some detail later. You will be astounded how important the Old Testament is in interpreting Revelation. Some scholars have identified more than two thousand allusions to the Old Testament. If you don't know the Old Testament background, you will not interpret Revelation very well.

6. Let the gospel transform the Old Testament.

Finally, we must learn to understand how the gospel transforms Old Testament images in the light of Jesus Christ. I can't emphasize this enough. John uses Old Testament images, but John is a first-century Christian, and he baptizes these Old Testament images into a Christian meaning. We'll get to more on this later. It's very important.

Structure of Revelation

Revelation is unique even among the prophetic books. Understanding a few things about the way Revelation was written will help us in our interpretations.

Revelation is not written like a novel, and it's not written sequentially (in logical order). I've heard it described as a mixed-up collage of pictures as opposed to a sequence of pictures. Statements sitting next to each other don't always relate to each other, which makes it difficult to see the overall picture in Revelation. However, in order to understand the details, we really have to see the big picture to know if the details even make sense.

Fortunately, even though things may seem mixed up on the surface, at least to our Western pattern of thinking, there is order in the book—in parallel structures. Learning to see the parallel structures in Revelation will help us. For example, the trumpet plagues and the bowl plagues affect the same things. They are separated by eight chapters of the book, but they are strongly related.

Or consider the two witnesses of chapter 11 and the land beast of chapter 13. One is on the side of God; the other is against him. But some fascinating connections emerge between them.

Also take note of Babylon and New Jerusalem: one is the city of Satan, and the other is the city of God. Yet there are strong parallels between them in Revelation.

We think differently

One of the reasons Revelation has this interesting structure is a cultural difference. Not all cultures think alike. Western logic in our culture is founded on Greek logic. Greek logic states that A+B=C. We think in terms of a beginning, middle, and end; an introduction, body, and conclusion. This is called linear logic. It goes in a straight line.

Hebrew logic from Bible times is different. Ancient Hebrew logic says that A+B=A-prime or A-expanded. It doesn't necessarily go in a straight line. We can best understand it as a mountain you climb. You are at point "A" at the foot of the mountain. You climb to point "B," which is the peak of the mountain, and then you climb down the other side. At the bottom of the other side of the mountain, you are again at point "A," but now you have been to the peak of the mountain and down again. You are no longer the same person you were before, so you are A-expanded. You can see the place you where you started in a new and better light.

If that doesn't make sense to you, it's OK. You were trained in Greek logic rather than Hebrew logic. To find the climax to a story using Greek logic, you go to the end. To find the climax in Hebrew logic, you look in the middle. The middle is the tipping point where everything changes.

Even though John wrote in Greek, he still thought in Hebrew logic. The book of Revelation is written with the structure that's common in Hebrew literature: the decisive portion of the book is located in the center, not at the end. This center is where we will be concentrating our efforts. In the middle of Revelation we find the final events leading up to the end of the world. Don't try to find them at the end of the book.

The structure of Revelation has a technical name. Scholars call it a *full-scale chiasm*. The Greek letter X denotes this structure, in which the first and last items compare, the second and next-to-last compare, and so on. The book of Revelation works its way from both ends of the book toward the center, kind of like burning a candle on both ends.

Look at the breakdown of the structure, going from the two ends to the middle:

- Prologue in 1:1–8 compares to Epilogue in 22:6–21
- Seven churches in 1:9–3:22 compares to New Jerusalem in 21:1–22:5
- Seven seals in 4:1–8:1 compare to millennium in 19:1–20:15
- Seven trumpets in 8:2–11:18 compare to seven bowls in 15:5–18:24
- Final crisis: 11:19–15:4

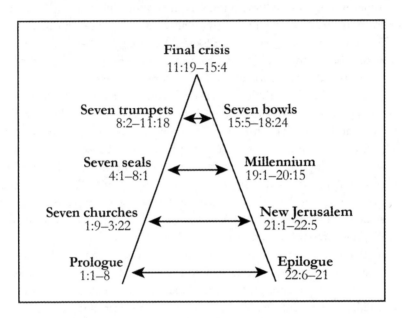

Figure 1 The structure of the book of Revelation

Pointing two directions

Another important structural element to understand about Revelation is that parts of it point forward and backward. In other words, the climax of one section of the book often serves as the introduction to the next section. Revelation drops hints of what the next passage means before you even get to it. Throughout the text of Revelation, you'll find embedded keys for unlocking the symbols.

1. Take, for example, Revelation 3:21. This is the end of a section, the climax to the letters to the seven churches, but it is also a complete introduction to the seven seals that come a few chapters later, describing the experiences of God's people from the time of the cross to the

second coming of Jesus. The verse works in two directions.

2. In Revelation 6:9–10, which is the end of a section—the climax to the fifth seal—the saints ask the question, "How long, Sovereign Lord, holy and true, until you judge the inhabitants of the earth and avenge our blood?" That question is answered later in Revelation 8:13: "Woe! Woe! Woe to the inhabitants of the earth, because of the trumpet blasts about to be sounded by the other three angels!" The trumpets are God's judgments on the wicked that the saints were pleading for in chapter 6. The verse works in two directions.

3. A particularly important example of a verse working in two directions is Revelation 12:17, which we will study in closer detail later. This verse ends the section of the sixth trumpet, but it also serves as the beginning of the final battle of earth's history.

Old Testament allusions

As mentioned before, to understand Revelation we must understand the Old Testament background of the book. The authors of the New Testament, including John, had been saturated in the Old Testament from childhood. Life revolved around religion, and their religion and culture were the same. Children memorized large portions of the Old Testament. The stories they grew up with were not Mother Goose and fairy tales. Their stories were David and Goliath and Moses and Elijah. The Old Testament was their lore. So it makes sense that the New Testament authors pulled from their history as they wrote. Revelation is interwoven with Old Testament imagery.

The New Testament writers referred to the Old Testament by allusion. An allusion is simply a reminder. The author uses a word, phrase, or name that reminds the reader of a particular detail or passage in another story. For example, if we mention 9/11 in a conversation, we need not say more. The term is loaded with meaning that everyone remembers. In the same way, whenever John referred to "Babylon," the word was loaded with meaning for his people. He didn't have to explain, because they knew.

Here's a quick experiment with a list of words. See if you get the allusions in them: Three Bears, Three Little Pigs, Cinderella, Pinocchio, Rapunzel, Rip Van Winkle, Sleeping Beauty, Humpty Dumpty, Jack and Jill, Ugly Duckling, Hansel and Gretel, Little Red Riding Hood. If you grew up in the United States, you probably know exactly which stories those words invoke. Why? Because we have a common background and grew up with the same stories. How long would it take for someone to tell all of those stories in detail? At least a couple of hours. But with a few key words, all of them leap to mind in just a few seconds.

If you went into the Amazon jungle and said to a tribal chief in his own language, "What big ears you have," would he have any clue what you were talking about? Well, yes and no. He would understand the literal meaning of your words because you spoke his language, but he would not understand your meaning. He wouldn't recognize the allusion to the story of Little Red Riding Hood.

Revelation has hundreds if not thousands of allusions to the Old Testament, and in this case *we* are the clueless ones. We understand the meaning of the individual words but do not understand their deeper meaning.

Being able to identify allusions in Revelation is vital to understanding it. To illustrate why this is so important, we'll use an example. Someone in your prophecy study group says, "I think that throne imagery in Revelation represents judgment." On the surface that might sound good. But when we track down the actual allusions, we find that throne imagery doesn't symbolize judgment at all. It symbolizes authority—a governing center, power, the one who is really in charge. Being able to identify allusions keeps us on the straight and narrow.

While taking Dr. Paulien's class I became excited about this idea of allusion. I thought it would be great to highlight in my Bible those passages in the Old Testament so that when reading them I could identify where they were pointing to in Revelation. I don't like highlighting in my Bible because it makes a mess, but I decided to make an exception. That was a mistake. Most of my Old Testament turned a brilliant highlighter yellow. I actually investigated and discovered that you can buy highlighter erasers. I bought a dozen of them and rescued my Bible.

However, before un-highlighting my Bible, I looked through and identified the yellowest sections and wrote them down in the list that follows. Learning your Old Testament by heart is no task for the faint of heart. It's a lot of work to know three-quarters of the Bible so intimately that a word or short phrase (an allusion) will immediately spark in your mind an entire context. What I discovered by highlighting my Bible was that if I could become intimately acquainted with some key sections of the Old Testament, then already I would be miles ahead in my understanding of Revelation.

So here's some valuable homework. Read and re-read the passages in the Old Testament listed below, with the idea in mind that Revelation alludes to these passages frequently. I've included some New Testament passages as well. Revelation doesn't allude to them, but they support the book in a significant way.

Old Testament passages to be familiar with:
- Genesis 3, 19
- Exodus 7, 10, 19, 20, 30
- Deuteronomy 32
- 1 Kings 17, 18
- Psalms 2, 29, 46, 79, 96, 114
- All of Isaiah, with special emphasis on chapters 11, 24, 34, 47–55, and 60–63
- Jeremiah 50, 51
- All of Ezekiel, with special emphasis on chapters 1, 4–6, 10, 14, 16, 26–29, and 37–39
- All of Daniel, with special emphasis on chapters 3 and 7–12
- Joel
- Nahum
- Zephaniah
- Zechariah 1–6, 12–14

Important New Testament passages to be familiar with:
- Matthew 24, 25
- Mark 13
- John 21
- 2 Thessalonians 2

Study Guide Outline

Chapter 4

1. Method for interpreting prophecy:

    a. Read _____ and broadly.

    b. Read the passage _____.

    c. Compare _____.

    d. Consider _____ relationships.

    e. Pay careful attention to the Old Testament _____.

    f. Try to understand how the Old Testament imagery is _____ by the gospel.

2. It's vital to understand the structure of Revelation in order to interpret it well.

    a. In a chiastic structure, the decisive portion is at the _____ of the book.

    b. Some verses of Revelation point both _____ and backward.

    c. Allusion is employed to direct a reader's mind to a larger _____ using just a word or phrase as a reminder.

    d. John alludes to the Old Testament _____ times in Revelation.

Chapter 5

Detecting Allusions

When I took the seminary class in the exegesis (interpretation) of Revelation and recognized the value of detecting allusions, I was nodding my head excitedly. This was great stuff. Then Dr. Paulien told us to go do it. Only then, he said, will you really get it. And he was right. I spent 30+ hours on three verses, tracking down the allusions. It was brutal work for someone who has no inclination toward being a scholar. But when I finished, I was a believer.

By now you should be convinced that detecting allusions is critical in understanding Revelation. John would have assumed that his readers would understand the big picture by the mention of a single word or phrase. When we don't have that past history, we are missing a huge piece of something we need in order to understand. Therefore, we must learn how to detect allusions. Since we don't have the history with the Old Testament the same way the Jews did, we have to investigate to understand. We do that by finding parallels with other scriptures that don't seem to be coincidental. Here is fair warning: it is work, but the reward is worth it.

For now we will hit only the high points of the process, and you can study it in greater detail in an appendix, "Detecting Allusions," at the end of the book. If you want serious training in this process, I recommend Jon Paulien's book *The Deep Things of God.*[5]

You have to be a pretty dedicated student of prophecy to do this right, because it does take significant time. But even if you don't do original research, you will have the tools to check on the work of others to see if it holds up to scrutiny.

Here, briefly, is how to detect allusions in Revelation. These are crucial tools that we will need later. We're going to be using all of them in the next section to identify things like the mark the beast and so on. You will want to fix these concepts in your mind.

---

5. Jon Paulien. *The Deep Things of God: An Insider's Guide to the Book of Revelation* (Hagerstown, MD: Review and Herald, 2004).

Step 1: Find verbal parallels in Revelation

If we can find our interpretations directly inside of Revelation, we have the strongest evidence that an interpretation is correct. So we begin by identifying verbal parallels within Revelation itself.

Once we have selected a portion of Revelation we want to interpret, we begin by marking the major words. Then we check to see if those words show up in other parts of Revelation. For instance, consider the word *testimony*. With some research we discover that it's found in both Revelation 1:9 and Revelation 6:9. Then after more comparison we find that a strong connection exists between those passages. We have just identified a parallel passage within the book of Revelation itself, which will yield a wealth of information.

Step 2: Find verbal parallels in the Old Testament

After we have tried to identify the parallels within Revelation itself, then we need to search for verbal parallels in the Old Testament. For instance, we might be interested in understanding more about the third angel's message in Revelation 14. We note some words in the passage that call on people to worship the God who made the heavens, the earth, the sea, and the springs of water. A search leads us to a strong verbal connection between that verse and the Ten Commandments in Exodus 20:8–11.

That's how you find verbal parallels. Again, you will find greater detail about the method in the appendix.

Step 3: Find Thematic Parallels

After we have identified verbal parallels, we then look for theme parallels, or parallel ideas. The evidence of what John intended becomes much stronger when we find two passages that have both words and ideas in common. For instance, as we will see in detail in section two of this book, in the first commandment we can identify an underlying salvation theme, in the second and third commandments we can identify an underlying judgment theme, and in the fourth commandment we can identify an underlying creation theme. Obviously, identifying themes requires deeper thinking than merely identifying words in common, but again, it's rewarding work.

Step 4: Structural parallels

Finally, after discovering thematic parallels, we seek structural parallels, which essentially ask the question, *Does this fit in the overall scheme of things?* A structural parallel in Revelation builds systematically on a part of the Old Testament. The structural parallel is one of the strongest indications that we have of an allusion. This will make more sense when we track down an example of a structural parallel later.

These steps are a method in a nutshell for detecting allusions in Revelation, and anywhere else in the Bible for that matter. We will be using this method as we get into the text of Revelation to help us interpret what we see there.

We're not going to leave out the New Testament, but John never alludes to the New Testament since it had not been put together when he wrote Revelation. So we will address that later.

At this point we get to delve into Revelation and try out our new tools to see where they lead us.

Study Guide Outline

Chapter 5

1. Being able to detect _____ in Revelation is critical to interpreting the book.

2. First try to detect allusions within Revelation by searching for _____ parallels.

3. Next, try to detect allusions in the Old Testament by searching for _____ parallels.

4. Next, search for _____ parallels.

5. Finally, search for _____ parallels.

Chapter 6

Revelation Is About Jesus

What is the first thing we usually think of when we hear the word *Revelation*? Is it beasts? The number 666? The antichrist? The strange symbols in Revelation are what most people think of first. But the first verse in the book says that it is the revelation of Jesus Christ.

If we read Revelation trying only to understand past or future events or to figure out the issues of the Middle East or other denominations or great wars or any other preconceived idea, then we're missing the entire point of the book. Revelation is about Jesus. So as we read and study, we must understand something about Jesus at every turn.

We may not see him in a cursory reading of the book, but if we dig more deeply we will find that Jesus is present everywhere. All of the New Testament writers saw pictures of Jesus throughout the Old Testament, and the author of Revelation is no exception. Nearly every chapter mentions Jesus directly in some way. The entire Old Testament and New Testament, especially the Gospels, meet and have their end in Revelation.

Since the New Testament writers were Christians, they would interpret everything they understood of the Old Testament as having been fulfilled in Jesus. We believe the same thing today.

Jesus replaces Old Testament characters

Before we get into the text of Revelation itself, we must recognize something vitally important for interpreting the book. As Christians the New Testament writers allowed the gospel to transform the Old Testament; it was expanded, enriched, and enlightened in Jesus.

Revelation and the rest of the New Testament present Jesus as the fulfillment of all sorts of Old Testament characters: Jesus as the new Adam, Jacob, Moses, Joshua, David, Solomon, Elisha, and so on. Why? Because apparently Jesus' life intentionally replicated a lot of Old Testament history for a very good reason.

To illustrate, let's look at Jesus as the new Adam. The New Testament writers describe Jesus as the second Adam, as Adam was originally created to be. Adam had been created in perfect relationship with God. He could walk and talk with Jesus face to face, as with a human friend. This was Adam's predestined way of life. But Adam chose to disobey God, and the relationship was broken.

Jesus came to earth as a second Adam and relived Adam's life as Adam had been predestined to live it. Jesus did this, first of all, to show us how to be human in the way God intended, and, second, he did this so that he could become the new leading representative of the human race.

In the beginning, Adam represented the entire human race. First Corinthians 15:22 tells us that one man's sin has affected all of us. "In Adam we all die." Adam represented the human race, and he made wrong choices. As a result, we, his descendants, have shared in the problem. However, the fact that Adam represented us is also good news, because as 1 Corinthians 15:22 goes on to say, "in [Jesus] Christ we all live."

So Jesus became the new representative of the human race when he replaced Adam's sinful past. And as our new representative Jesus is able to replace our defective past as well. Not just cover it up, mind you, but replace it. Is that good news or what! That is why the definition of *gospel* is "good news." In Christ, we are not just refurbished equipment. We are brand new people. Our old sinful selves are dead, buried, and gone. We are recreated in the image of God.[6]

Because Jesus replaced Adam, he can stand before God the Father and plead our case *as us*, because he is our representative. When we accept him as our Savior, he becomes our righteousness (right-ness). Outside of Jesus Christ, we are the first Adam, fallen and cursed by our own choice. But when we're in Jesus, when standing before God the Father we *are* Jesus, because we are covered completely by him. That's the good news of grace! That is the grand story of redemption. Words are simply inadequate to state this well.

But the story goes deeper. In replacing our lost and sinful condition, Jesus also took on himself the consequences of our failure. In order for

---

6. This, by the way, is the entire point of the symbolism of baptism. When we decide that we will in fact commit our lives to Christ, we die symbolically to ourselves, we are buried in the waters of baptism, then we are raised again into new life in Jesus Christ.

God to be just in his mercy, someone had to pay the penalty for our wrong choices—our sin. So even though Jesus relived Adam's messed-up life without messing up himself, he still accepted the consequences for Adam's sin.

After Adam disobeyed God, he was cursed with several things: thorns in the ground, the sweat of hard labor, nakedness, and death (see Genesis 3). When Jesus died, that is what he suffered as well: thorns, sweat, nakedness, and death. This is not coincidental, which will become clear the more we go on.

By his perfect life as a human being, Jesus redeemed Adam's history and ours, and yet he also bore the consequences of our failure in order to give us a right to his perfect life. This way, God was merciful and just at the same time. He was merciful because Jesus came to our place (the earth), and just because he died in our place.

There are two reasons for talking about Jesus' redemption of Adam's history. First, it is great news. You don't have to be the person you are now or that you have been. In Jesus your past can be completely replaced. The second reason is because this idea profoundly affects how we interpret Revelation.

Jesus as the new Israel

Jesus relived another Old Testament story as well. After Adam failed, God raised up an entire nation to help restore what Adam destroyed. God's specific purpose in creating the nation of Israel was to show the world how to live in relationship with him. The people were to bring the world and God back together and help to restore the relationship that Adam had broken. Unfortunately, Israel failed to live up to its intended purpose. So Jesus also relived the history of the entire nation of Israel.

This isn't just interesting; it is crucial for our study. Jesus was much more than just a new Adam. He was also a new Jacob (aka Israel), a new Moses (Israel's first leader), a new Joshua (Israel's second leader), a new David (Israel's greatest king), a new Solomon (Israel's wisest king), a new Elisha (Israel's prophet), and even a new Cyrus (Israel's deliverer from Babylonian captivity). All of these people played important roles in the life of the Old Testament nation of Israel.

Just look at some of the parallels between Jesus' life and Israel's history:

1. Moses, as an infant, narrowly escaped being killed by an evil king, just

as Jesus did.

2. Moses fasted 40 days in the wilderness, as did Jesus.
3. Moses appointed 70 elders; Jesus sent out 70 disciples.
4. Israel went from Canaan to Egypt and back to Canaan, and Jesus did the same thing.
5. Israel came through the waters of the Red Sea and then went into the wilderness; Jesus came through the waters of baptism and then went into the wilderness.
6. Israel spent 40 years in the wilderness; Jesus spent 40 days in the wilderness.
7. Israel had 12 tribes, and Jesus chose 12 disciples.

The parallels go on to the point that it's difficult to believe these are coincidences. Jesus relived Israel's life and thereby *became* the new Israel. He became the new Adam to show us how to live in relationship to God. And he became the new Israel to show us how to reconcile others to God.

After living that life perfectly, Jesus took upon himself the consequences for Israel's failure.

Deuteronomy 28 is specific about the consequences for failure. Among the curses outlined were

1. Being stripped of wealth and living in poverty. That describes Jesus, with not even a place to "lay his head."
2. Israel's failure meant being killed by their enemies. Jesus was killed by his enemies.
3. Israel's failure would result in being mocked, thirsty, and left naked and in the dark. On the cross Jesus experienced all of those: darkness, mocking, thirst, nakedness.
4. Israel's failure would result in an anxious mind and despairing heart, which well describes Jesus in the garden of Gethsemane the night before he died.

Put all of the curses beside Jesus' experience, and you will find that he went through every one of them so that he could become the new Israel.

The church modeled on the experience of Jesus

In Revelation the fact that Jesus became the new Israel is extremely significant. Here's why. Just as we immediately recognize "what big ears you have" and understand its context, the early Christians would have recognized the statement John makes in Revelation 5:10, referring to God's end-time people: "You have made them to be a kingdom and priests to serve our God and they will reign on the earth."

The Christians of John's day would have recognized immediately the distinct allusion to Exodus 19:5, 6, which says, " 'Now if you obey me fully and keep my covenant, then out of all nations you will be my treasured possession. Although the whole earth is mine, you will be for me a kingdom of priests and a holy nation.' " In Exodus these words are spoken to Israel. In Revelation they are spoken to the Christians in the seven churches.

The implications of this are mind-boggling. God originally founded the nation of Israel to be a kingdom of priests, with the function of helping to reconcile the sinful world to God. But Israel failed at this purpose. Now John, one of Jesus' closest disciples, transfers in one fell swoop the responsibilities of the nation of Israel onto the new Israel, the Christian church—including you and me.

Now wait a minute! Why would John do that? Isn't Jesus the one who relived Israel's history? Yes, but he is not the only one. When we look at the history of the Christian church since Jesus was on earth, the experience of the church is a parallel of the life of Jesus when he became the new Israel.

Again, take a look at the parallels between Israel, Jesus, and the Christian church:

1. In Revelation 12: The saints go into the wilderness (Revelation 12:6, 14), as did Israel and Jesus.

2. In Revelation 6: The saints are put to death (Revelation 6:9, 10), as Israel and Jesus were.

3. In Revelation 13: The saints endure suffering (Revelation 13: 9, 10; 12:14), as did Israel and Jesus.

4. In Revelation 1 and 5: The saints are kings and priests (Revelation 1:5, 6; 5:9, 10), just as Israel and Jesus were.

5. In Revelation 11: The saints serve 1,260 days clothed in sackcloth (Revelation 11:3), just as Jesus' ministry was 1,260 days, or three and a half years (using the Israelites' calendar).

6. In Revelation 11: the saints are slain and mocked (Revelation 11:7–10), just as Jesus was.

7. In Revelation 11: The saints are resurrected and ascend to heaven (Revelation 11:11, 12), just like Jesus.

So Revelation is describing, simultaneously, the experience of Jesus as the new Israel and the experience of his true church from the cross to the Second Coming. The experiences are parallel in too many ways to be coincidental.

Why go into such depth on this point? Because it is vital to understanding the book of Revelation. In Revelation, Israel is not a literal nationality or ethnicity, because Revelation, and the New Testament, expand the definition of Israel to mean Jesus Christ and his church.[7]

Some people call this "replacement theology" and are offended by it. It's really expansion theology, for which we Gentiles (people who aren't Jewish) should be incredibly grateful. From the beginning, God planned to save us all, not replace some of us with others. It's important to understand that in Revelation, Israel represents God's people in the Christian church. Miss this one point and we might as well quit trying to understand Revelation. When we read about Israel in Revelation, we must not think of it as the literal nation of Israel. Nor should we think that it means Israel as a geographic area, because the new Israel (Jesus) is located in heavenly places (see Revelation 5:6–14; 7:15–17), not in the Middle East. It doesn't take long comparing the book of Zechariah to Revelation to see that when John speaks of Jerusalem, he sees it as representing the world, not a specific geographic location (compare Zechariah 12:10 with Revelation 1:7).

So even though Revelation uses Old Testament language about Israel and its neighbors, its significance is neither ethnic nor geographical in this case. When Revelation speaks of Israel, it is a symbol of all God's faithful people everywhere (including believers who happen to be Jewish by birth).

As we study further in Revelation, it will become obvious that Babylon is symbolic also. It cannot be a reference to a literal city in Iraq but is rather a religious movement that fights against Jesus. There are many more examples of places and nations as spiritual symbols, and our conclusion must be that the book of Revelation treats Israel, its neighbors, and even Babylon in a symbolic spiritual sense.

Spirituality is always synonymous with relationship. Pardon my blunt-

---

7. It is redundant to say "Jesus Christ and his church," because the Bible puts those two things together as one. Christ is the head, and his church is his body. You don't refer to yourself as your head and your body. You are one, and Jesus and the church are one.

ness, but anyone who considers themselves spiritual but does not spend time working on a daily, growing, intentional relationship with Jesus is fooling themselves about their own spirituality. The depth of spirituality is always directly proportional to the depth of relationship.

The entire key to understanding Revelation, just as it is with the rest of the Bible, is to see it in the light of relationship to Jesus Christ. The book of Revelation is the revelation of Jesus. If we think that the book of Revelation is taking us anywhere else, we know that we have steered away from the true intent of the book. The evidence for this will pile up high as we go on.

Study Guide Outline

Chapter 6

1. Revelation is about _____.

2. Jesus became the new Adam in order to become the new _____ of the human race.

3. Even though Jesus relived Adam's life perfectly, he still accepted the _____ of Adam's failure.

4. Jesus _____ my sinful past with his perfect life.

5. Jesus also relived the history of _____ _____ Israel.

6. Even though Jesus relived Israel's history perfectly, he still accepted the _____ of Israel's failure.

7. In doing this, Jesus _____ the new Israel.

8. Revelation 5:10 places on the new Israel the _____ of Old Testament Israel: Christ and his church.

9. In Revelation, references to Israel cannot refer to _____ or _____ or _____.

10. References to Israel in Revelation refer to _____ Israel.

11. The entire key to understanding Revelation is to see it in the light of _____ to Jesus Christ.

Chapter 7

Prologue of Revelation

> The revelation of Jesus Christ, which God gave him to show his servants what must soon take place. He made it known by sending his angel to his servant John, who testifies to everything he saw—that is, the word of God and the testimony of Jesus Christ. Blessed is the one who reads the words of this prophecy, and blessed are those who hear it and take to heart what is written in it, because the time is near. —Revelation 1:1–3

It's surprising to see what we can learn from the introduction to Revelation. Some of us are used to jumping right to Revelation 13 to figure out who the beast is, or Revelation 16 to figure out what Armageddon is all about. We virtually ignore the stage-setting introduction. But understanding a few things in the introduction will safeguard us from making incorrect assumptions about what we will encounter later.

First, in verse 1, we are told the overall purpose of the book of Revelation. The purpose is to show to his servants (God's people) what is going to happen soon. Revelation's purpose is to unfold the future for us in the context of Jesus Christ.

That is the baseline. Everything we attempt to understand in Revelation must make sense in this overall purpose.

Daniel and Revelation have a special connection

If we're willing to do some investigating with the method we've already discussed, we will find a strong allusion to the Old Testament in this introduction, specifically to Daniel 2. Consider some significant parallel words in the original Greek of Revelation and in the Septuagint, which is the Greek translation of the Old Testament. The first is *dei genesthai*, "what must happen."

This is an unusual phrase in Scripture, so when we see it in Daniel 2 it should catch our attention. It's the first evidence of a special connection between Revelation and Daniel, which we're going to see time and time again.

Another instance of this phrase occurs in Daniel 2:28. "There is a God in heaven who reveals mysteries. He has shown King Nebuchadnezzar what will happen in days to come." In this passage, God "showed Nebuchadnezzar what must happen [*dei genesthai*][8] in the last days." In Revelation 1 God showed John what must happen shortly or soon. What Daniel saw in the distant future, John saw would happen soon.

But *dei genesthai* is just the first parallel between these verses. The connection gets stronger. In the second part of verse 1, we find the word *esaymanen*, which means "signified." "He sent and signified it by his angel unto his servant John" (KJV). Other translations use the words *shown* or *revealed* or *communicated*. But *signified* is probably the best translation.

In Daniel 2:45, we see the same interesting word. "The great God has shown [*esaymanen*] to the king what will take place in the future [*eschaton*]." *Eschatos* is the Greek word from which we get our word *eschaton*, referring not to just any time in the future but specifically to the time of the end of the world. So God signified to John and Nebuchadnezzar what must take place in the time of the end. What about that word *signify*? What does it mean?

The golden arches signify McDonalds. We call it a logo, but it's also a symbol. It signifies the company. In ancient times, a king used a signet ring pressed into hot wax to signify that he was approving a law or proclamation. We each have a signature, which signifies our approval or endorsement. The word *signifies* is found in John 12, where Jesus points to the snake that Moses raised in the wilderness as a symbol of his death for our sins.

In the books of Revelation and Daniel, God is "signifying" things. In other words, he is showing by symbols what will happen in the future. The more we compare the two books, the more we'll realize that Revelation is explaining the symbols of the book of Daniel.

This connection has several implications. First, if we don't connect the book of Daniel with Revelation, we will be severely handicapped as we try to understand Revelation. Daniel's prophecies find their ultimate fulfillment in Revelation. The two are companion volumes.

---

8. Old Testament references to Greek come from the Septuagint, the Greek translation of the Old Testament.

A second implication is that since the visions in Daniel point to the end of time, and Revelation explains the visions of Daniel, then Revelation truly does deal with the time of the end, and not the past as some interpreters claim.

Consider also that the wording we see at the beginning of Revelation and in Daniel we also see in Jesus' sermons on the end time, such as in Matthew 24. If we want to understand Revelation, we must take into account Daniel's visions and Jesus' sermons concerning the last days.

Now let's go back to the word *esaymanen*, or "signified." The word denotes a cryptic symbolic vision. The golden arches are not the actual McDonalds; they are only a cryptic symbol or a code. The only reason we know the meaning of the symbol is that the McDonalds company spends lots of money making sure people everywhere know the meaning of it.

In Revelation 1:1 God has signified, or shown using symbols, what will happen at the end of time. Revelation wants us to know from the beginning that the book is not your typical, literal New Testament book. Rather, it is packed with symbols.

Symbolism is default mode

If you have ever heard that Revelation should be understood literally, we have just seen in detail that this is not possible. Symbolism is the rule for Revelation rather than the exception. Considering how clearly this is stated, it seems odd that people sometimes debate this issue. Right in the first verse we're told point blank that Revelation is a book of symbols.

When we interpret the rest of the Bible, we work the other way around. We assume something is literal unless there are compelling reasons to believe it's symbolic. Revelation works in precisely the opposite way. At the very beginning we are told that we are to understand Revelation as symbolic unless there is a compelling reason to believe that it is literal.

Of course, some symbolic things appear in other New Testament books, just as there are some literal things in Revelation. But the default mode is symbolism in Revelation. This will be a safeguard to us as we interpret Revelation.

Revelation is about the future

What was signified, according to verse 1, were the things that must soon take place. From John's point of view, Revelation clearly concerns the future, and in connection with Daniel, not just any time in the future but specifically the time of the end. This has major implications for some popular interpretations of Revelation.

John didn't make up Revelation

John didn't dream up the book of Revelation on his own. According to the first verse, God signified the book and gave it to Jesus, who then gave it to John through his angel. John used his own words, but the symbols John saw and described belong to God. This also has implications for interpretation.

Revelation was written to be understood

Some claim that Revelation is a sealed book and cannot be understood. Let's go on in the introduction and see if that holds up. "Blessed is the one who reads the words of this prophecy, and blessed are those who hear it and take to heart what is written in it, because the time is near" (Revelation 1:3). A couple of significant things appear in this verse.

First, it seems that the book of Revelation was intended to be read out loud ("blessed is he who reads") with people listening to it ("blessed are those who hear"). It was written to the seven churches, so the book of Revelation was originally intended to be read aloud in the seven churches.

The Greek word for "hear" has different meanings depending on its object. If the object is accusative, it means to hear with understanding. If its object is genitive, it means to hear without understanding. Here the object is accusative, which means the blessing is for those who hear and *understand* the words of the prophecy. So for those who say Revelation can't be understood, verse 3 tells us otherwise.

Some also say that Revelation can only be understood by us, and that those in the past could not understand it. But the blessing was pronounced on the people in the seven churches who heard and understood. Revelation had a message to the original readers and hearers, which is an important consideration we must reckon with in our own interpretation. They understood the symbols of 666, Armageddon, the beast, and so on.

Study Guide Outline

Chapter 7

1. The purpose of Revelation is to show God's people what is going to happen _____.

2. There is a special connection between _____ and Revelation.

3. Revelation is concerned with the time of the _____.

4. In understanding Revelation we must take into account Daniel's _____ and Jesus' words concerning the last days.

5. _____ is the rule for Revelation, not literalism. It is the default mode.

6. John didn't _____ Revelation; he wrote down what Jesus showed him.

7. Revelation was intended to be _____ by us and those in the past.

Section 2
Deciphering the
Battle of Armageddon

Chapter 8

A Particular People Who Will Deliver an End-Time Message

Revelation 10

Now we switch gears from filling up our interpretation toolboxes to using those tools to interpret the prophecy of Revelation 10. Revelation 10 is not as dramatic as the fearsome beasts of Revelation 13 or Armageddon in Revelation 16. But Revelation 10 is a wonderful chapter because it is where prophecy reveals a particular group of people at the end of time who will deliver a specific final message to the world. It identifies who the group is, when they will deliver, and what their message is going to be.

> I saw another mighty angel coming down from heaven. He was robed in a cloud, with a rainbow above his head; his face was like the sun, and his legs were like fiery pillars. He was holding a little scroll, which lay open in his hand. He planted his right foot on the sea and his left foot on the land, and he gave a loud shout like the roar of a lion. When he shouted, the voices of the seven thunders spoke (Revelation 10:1–3).

This isn't the first time we see an angel with a scroll in Revelation. In Revelation 5 John sees the angel holding a closed scroll. Now in Revelation 10 he sees that the scroll is opened. Also in Daniel 12 there is another angel with a scroll that remained closed up "until the time of the end." We already have good reason to suspect a connection. But let's see how the scene in Revelation plays out first.

> Then the angel I had seen standing on the sea and on the land raised his right hand to heaven. And he swore by

him who lives for ever and ever, who created the heavens and all that is in them, the earth and all that is in it, and the sea and all that is in it, and said, "There will be no more delay! But in the days when the seventh angel is about to sound his trumpet, the mystery of God will be accomplished, just as he announced to his servants the prophets" (verses 5–7).

The angel says, "There will be no more delay." The word *delay* is actually an interpretation of the original Greek, which means the translators had some choices to make when they translated the word. Greek has more than one word for time. There is *chyros*, which is a specific or an appointed time. Christmas, for example, is a *chyros* time. The other Greek word for time is *chronos*, from which we get our words like chronology and chronometer. The word *chronos* means the passage of time. In the original language the angel is recorded as saying, "There will be no more *chronos*." In other words, there will be no more passage of time.

Remember that allusion is the primary way that John calls our attention to a specific context in the Old Testament. In this passage we encounter a strong allusion to Daniel 12. So we take out our verbal parallel tool. Pay close attention to the italicized words.

"But you, Daniel, close up and *seal the words of the scroll* until the time of the end. Many will go here and there to increase knowledge." Then I, Daniel, looked, and there before me stood two others, one on this bank of the river and one on the opposite bank. One of them said to the *man clothed in linen*, who was *above the waters of the river*, "How long will it be before these astonishing things are fulfilled?"

The man clothed in linen, *who was above the waters of the river, lifted his right hand and his left hand toward heaven, and I heard him swear* by him who lives forever, saying, "It will be for a time, times and half a time. When the power of the holy people has been finally broken, all these things will be completed" (Daniel 12:4–7).

If we lay these passages in Revelation 10 and Daniel 12 side by side, we can pretty easily see the parallels. This is such a clear verbal parallel that it's almost a direct quotation. There are also structural parallels, which is another tool in our interpretation toolbox. The passage in Revelation is obviously building *systematically* on the passage in Daniel 12. There are some significant differences, however; and it's these differences we will want to notice. The scroll in Daniel 12 is closed, and in Revelation 10, it's open.

So we have several questions at this point. Could it be that these verses in Revelation 10 are talking about the time to open the closed scroll of Daniel—the sealed prophecies of Daniel? Or, like some have thought, is the passage about the Second Coming? Or is it perhaps about when the time prophecies of Daniel come to an end? Let's employ our Bible interpretation tools.

Notice that Daniel 12 mentions a location: above the waters of the river. It also mentions raising the right hand to heaven and swearing an oath. In Revelation 10 there's a location: standing on land and on sea, raising right hand to heaven, and swearing an oath. Clearly the scenes are structurally parallel.

The significant difference between them is in what the angel swears. In Daniel 12 he swears, "Time, times and half a time." In Revelation 10 he swears, "There will be no more delay." No more *chronos*. Revelation 10 is replaying the scene of Daniel 12, but now the scroll that had been sealed for Daniel is open for John. In Revelation 5, you may recall, the Lamb who was worthy opened the sealed scroll. It's all connected. The scroll Daniel had seen was sealed shut until the time of the end; therefore, Revelation 10 is located at whatever time Daniel meant by the time of the end. Good detective work going on here.

So in order for us to understand Revelation 10, Daniel 12 is a crucial passage. But Daniel 12 is also a key passage in the book of Daniel itself. It's the climax of an entire sequence that begins all the way back in Daniel 8. So when John alludes to Daniel 12, he has something much bigger in mind than simply alluding to this one scene of the angel above the river. John knew the entire story in Daniel and knew his readers did too. It would be like my saying to you that "the porridge was just right," and you would immediately recognize the allusion to Goldilocks and the three bears. But in that allusion, you wouldn't limit yourself to just remembering the scene of Goldilocks sampling the porridge; you instantaneously incorporate the entire story into what you hear me saying.

This is a perfect example of how a deeper understanding of the book of Daniel is necessary to interpreting Revelation. Daniel 12 is the climax to a long story that began in Daniel 8 when the little horn power begins to persecute and kill God's people. The question comes up, "How long will it take for this vision to be fulfilled?" The answer comes back, "2,300 days until the sanctuary is cleansed." But then no further explanation is given. So we are left wondering what the 2,300 days are all about.

A few years later, an angel comes to Daniel and gives more explanation for the 2,300-day time prophecy, but once again he doesn't give a full explanation. Then the prophet gets a little more information later, in Daniel 12, but then he is told to seal up the vision because it concerns the time of the end. Daniel never did understand this sealed prophecy.

John recognized in his vision the allusion to the overall context of Daniel's 2,300-day time prophecy. He recognized that what he was seeing in his vision was expanding on what Daniel had seen. He was seeing the time in the future when the 2,300-day time prophecy would finally be unlocked and understood.

Daniel's time prophecies unsealed

Many of Daniel's visions were easy to understand because the angel explained them outright. But no one could make heads or tails of the time prophecies for thousands of years. The angel told Daniel the prophecy would be sealed (closed up) until the time of the end.

This prediction came true. In the 1800s, William Miller figured out the 2,300-day prophecy. Unfortunately, he and his colleagues thought the phrase "there will be no more delay" meant that they had reached the time of the Second Coming and that Jesus would be coming back on the particular date when the 2,300-day prophecy ended.

Likely they didn't recognize in their English translation that the predicted event was not a *chyros* event—not a specific time that had arrived. Instead it was the end of the definite *chronos*, the end of the time prophecies that could be calculated.

It was an easy mistake to make. Look again at Revelation 10:6. "And he swore by him who lives for ever and ever, who created the heavens and all that is in them, the earth and all that is in it, and the sea and all that is in it, and said, 'There will be no more delay!' "

The first impression we get is that when the time prophecies end, that is the end of everything. But what follows immediately after counters that impression. "But in the days when the seventh angel is about to sound his trumpet, the mystery of God will be accomplished, just as he announced to his servants the prophets" (Revelation 10:7). When the time prophecies of Daniel close, it seems logical to expect the end, but something else happens in instead. The mystery of God is finished. The mystery of God is something that happens between the time when Daniel's time prophecies end and the time of the seventh angel blowing his trumpet, which will bring on the Second Coming.

The next logical question, of course, is what is the mystery of God? Scholars of all backgrounds generally agree on this point. The Greek wording is pretty clear. It is *eueggelisn* (pronounced *evengelisn*), from which we get our word *evangelism*. The mystery of God is the preaching of the gospel.

This lines up with Jesus' prediction in Matthew 24:14 that the gospel will go to the whole world just before the end. It also lines up with Revelation 14:6, which describes the message going to the world just before judgment arrives.

What we are seeing is that an unknown period of time will elapse between the end of the time prophecies of Daniel (the end of the 2,300 days) and the second coming of Christ. During this time there will be no definite tracing of prophetic time as there had been up to that point. Thus, no man knows the day or the hour that Jesus will come back. We cannot predict any date for when Jesus will return. But we know a time comes when the book of Daniel makes complete sense, when the 2,300-day prophecy is understood—the time that Daniel called the time of the end.

John was seeing that during the time of the end, people would study Bible prophecy on a large scale. And the reality is that Daniel and Revelation have never been studied on a larger scale than they have in the past couple of hundred years. I have heard that more has been written on end-time prophecy in the past 30 years than in the previous two thousand. This fits what we are seeing in Revelation 10 in the final proclamation of the end-time message.

Daniel's time prophecy ended in the 1800s—in 1844 to be exact. It's important to trace those prophecies and be familiar with them, but that has been done enough in other books. Suffice to say that we are living in the period called the time of the end. The time of the end isn't the final end. Think of it like a movie. The time of the end of the movie is the final minutes, the climax of the film. The very end comes when the credits roll.

We are living in the time of the end, the final moments, the climax to the drama, when the mystery of God is being finished. The special gospel message is right now going to the world, and this will take an unspecified amount of time. The next thing on the schedule, as soon as this message has gone out to the whole world, is that Jesus will return.

Imagine how the Millerites (William Miller and his followers) must have felt when they finally realized that the prophecy puzzle of the 2,300 days had finally been solved. They must have been ecstatic. It located them in history. What a time to be alive! These prophecies concern our time, right now. And that sense of where we stand in history is an energizing force to finish spreading the message to the world so that Jesus can return. It gives us a sense of mission and purpose.

We cannot predict when Jesus will come, but He has shown us that we are living in earth's last days. This final era in which we live is the major focus from chapter 10 to the end of the book of Revelation.

Let's look at more in Revelation 10.

> Then the voice that I had heard from heaven spoke to me once more: "Go, take the scroll that lies open in the hand of the angel who is standing on the sea and on the land." So I went to the angel and asked him to give me the little scroll. He said to me, "Take it and eat it. It will turn your stomach sour, but in your mouth it will be as sweet as honey." I took the little scroll from the angel's hand and ate it. It tasted as sweet as honey in my mouth, but when I had eaten it, my stomach turned sour. Then I was told, "You must prophesy again about many peoples, nations, languages and kings" (Revelation 10:8–11 NIV).

Here John participates in the vision as he acts out a small parable. What is happening comes in response to his excitement about the news he had just received concerning earth's final era. John must have understood the implications of what he was seeing and hearing. Jesus' return must be just around the corner! So what happens next is the response to John's joy.

Obediently John takes the scroll from the angel and eats it. Just as he had been warned, it tasted sweet in his mouth but made his stomach bitter. The experience mirrored the emotions John would have to go through. At first he was overjoyed at receiving this vision. Maybe he thought that as soon as he wrote this out, the effect would be so great that it would bring on the end of time immediately. That was a sweet thought!

But then the next words John hears are bitter to his high hopes. "You must prophesy again." In other words, "No, John, this isn't going to be what you expect. Christians will have to go out and preach some more. This is not the end." After he gained such high hopes, this was bitter news. This sweet/bitter experience may have been what happened to John, but more than that, it was a prophecy about the situation to occur later, in the 1800s.

Unbeknownst to John, he had acted out the experience of the Millerites in the 1800s when they studied Daniel's time prophecies. Like John, they thought, *The end is nearly here!* They had it figured out, down to the day, when the 2,300-day prophecy would end. This would be when the sanctuary was cleansed, which they thought meant the return of Jesus. What a sweet thought. They were so adamant about the coming second advent of Jesus that people started calling them adventists rather than Millerites.

In the end the sweetness was bitterness to them. Jesus didn't come back in 1844. They had the time prophecies right, but they didn't understand the meaning of the cleansing of the sanctuary. They soon realized that they had to go out and prophesy again. They had to continue preaching. It slowly dawned on these adventists that they had been identified in Revelation 10 as the people who must go out and finish the mystery of God.

These were a special group of God's end-time people. During the "delay" time, when there are no more time prophecies, John saw that a particular group of people would understand the time prophecies of Daniel and would be bitterly disappointed when Jesus didn't come as they expected, and that they would come out of that disappointment and prophesy again—they would hit the evangelism trail. They were the ones who would finish the work of taking the gospel to the entire world just before the final events of earth's history.

The final message of God's end-time people

So what will be the final message that this group delivers? What else could it be but the gospel, which is to go to the whole world before the end comes? And what else could it be but that gospel preached in light of the prophecies concerning the time of the end? The message of God's final messengers has to be the gospel with special relevance to the last days.

This understanding must profoundly influence how we structure our preaching and teaching. The prophecy is a directive for the time in history in which we live. It's a responsibility of God's people to bring these prophecies to light so that the world will recognize the times in which we live. However, we must do it with a gospel focus.

It's tempting when preaching prophecy for us to concentrate on symbols, sensational interpretations, ugly beasts, and ferocious wars. But those bearing the final message must avoid that focus. Instead we must focus on sharing prophecy in a way that reveals Jesus Christ, in a way that make a difference in people's lives for the last days.

Of course, focusing only on sensational beasts and ferocious wars is just one extreme. The other extreme is to say, "Let's just focus on the gospel and ignore prophecy." But if we understand Revelation 10 correctly, the final message is a blending of prophecy and gospel. When Jesus is lifted up alongside those prophecies and God's people find great power in that combination, they will have the final message that must be carried to the world. We might say that these prophecies are an indispensable *part* of the gospel.

The sanctuary

But wait! There is one more thing that will be a part of this end-time message, and it's found in the next two verses that begin in Revelation 11. These verses would fit better in chapter 10, but that's not the way it was divided. The chapter and verse divisions were not inspired; they were merely added to make reference easier.

Revelation 11:1–2 continues the acted parable in which John was participating. He ate the sweet scroll; it turned bitter; he's told to prophesy some more; and then the angel hands him a reed, an old-fashioned tape measure if you will.

"I was given a reed like a measuring rod and was told, 'Go and measure the temple of God and the altar, and count the worshipers there. But exclude the outer court; do not measure it, because it has been given to the Gentiles. They will trample on the holy city for 42 months' " (Revelation 11:1–2).

"You must prophesy again," the angel tells John, and then hands him a measuring rod to measure the temple of God and the altar, and tells him to count the worshipers there. After both John and the Millerites of the 1800s were so excited and then disappointed, they were directed to a closer study of the sanctuary, in order to help them understand what they had misunderstood before. The Old Testament sanctuary and the way it operated would provide them the clues and the answers they needed to understand what was going on and why things had happened they way they did.

The Millerites eventually recognized this, and by studying the Old Testament sanctuary they discovered what the cleansing of the sanctuary was all about. It referred to the Day of Atonement, a time of judgment for Israel in the Old Testament and for the world in the New Testament. With this combination of gospel, prophecy, and the explanation of the sanctuary, they had the complete message that they were to carry to the world for the last days.

So out of their great disappointment this group of adventists found new life when they identified themselves in Revelation 10. When is the last time you heard that message—a blending of prophecy, gospel, and sanctuary? If what we're seeing here is true, then we should be looking for and joining those who are sharing that message. They exist. If you are serious about being a part of the movement of God's end-time messengers, find those who are delivering this message, and deliver it yourself.

Study Guide Outline

Chapter 8

1. Revelation 10 identifies a special group of _____ who will carry a special message, and _____ they will do it.

2. Revelation 10 and Daniel 12 are _____ passages.

3. In Daniel 12 the scroll is _____. In Revelation 10 the scroll is open.

4. Daniel 12 is the _____ to a prophecy that begins in Daniel 8.

5. In Revelation 10 John is taking into account the entire _____ of the vision from Daniel 8–12.

6. Only the time prophecies of Daniel aren't explained in Daniel. They are the "_____" prophecies.

7. The open scroll in Revelation 10 symbolizes the time when Daniel's _____ prophecies would be understood.

8. "There will be no more delay," means "there will be no more _____ prophecies."

9. After the time prophecies end, then the _____ of God will be finished.

10. The mystery of God is the _____ going to the whole world.

11. There will be an _____ period of time between the end of the time prophecies of Daniel and the second coming of Christ.

12. God's end-time special messengers are those who _____ the time prophecies.

13. They bring a special _____ during the time of the end, the time when the mystery of God is being finished.

14. This special message will include:

    a.   _____

    b.   _____

    c.   _____

    d.   With special _____ to the last days.

Chapter 9

Three Stages of Christian History

Revelation 12

There appears to be something of a system in Revelation. Each time a new character is introduced, the narrative pauses to describe that character. For instance, when Jesus is first introduced in chapter 1, John describes him as walking among seven lampstands, dressed in a robe to his feet with a golden sash, white hair, eyes like fire, feet like glowing bronze, and so on. After that, whenever Jesus is depicted, even if he is called by another name or pictured by another symbol like a lamb or a lion or a rider on a horse, Revelation does not re-describe him.

A cursory reading of Revelation reveals what appear to be many characters, when in reality there are just a few characters known by different names and symbols. Generally speaking, each character is introduced and described only once, so if we encounter a character we don't recognize and it is not described, then it's quite possible that we have encountered this character before under a different name or symbol. Keep this in mind in Revelation 12 and 13.

Revelation 12 reveals a prophetic overview of Christian history, a sequence of events with cosmic implications. The verses aren't in perfect sequential order, so we have to follow closely. But if we're willing to study it out, we will see three stages of the history of the Christian church emerge from the text. The first two stages for us are history, and the third stage will take place sometime in the near future.

> A great and wondrous sign appeared in heaven: a woman clothed with the sun, with the moon under her feet and a crown of twelve stars on her head. She was pregnant and cried out in pain as she was about to give birth. Then another sign appeared in heaven: an enormous red dragon with seven heads and ten horns and seven crowns on his heads. His tail swept a third of the stars out of the sky

> and flung them to the earth. The dragon stood in front of the woman who was about to give birth, so that he might devour her child the moment it was born. She gave birth to a son, a male child, who will rule all the nations with an iron scepter. And her child was snatched up to God and to his throne. The woman fled into the desert to a place prepared for her by God, where she might be taken care of for 1,260 days (Revelation 12:1–6).

John saw a woman in the heavens who was pregnant. Also in the heavens was a great red dragon that was obviously the enemy of the woman and the child she was about to bear. That dragon was prepared to devour the child as soon as it was born. A male child was born, but the child was caught up to God and to his throne.

Three characters are in play here. First, a woman whom most scholars agree represents, in some form or another, the people of God. Some say it is specifically Israel, some say it is Eve or Mary, some say the Christian church, but most everyone agrees that at least in some sense, the woman represents the people of God.

The Eve or Mary scenarios don't hold up because we're looking at symbols instead of literal people. Also, in verse 6, this woman symbolically flees to the desert for an amount of time that is longer than a person's lifetime. That fact alone rules out a specific person. It makes more sense that this woman is a symbol of the people of God.

The second character is an enormous red dragon whose identity is given outright in verse 9. The great dragon is Satan, the devil.

The third character is the male child, and again, most everyone agrees that the child is Jesus because He is to rule with an iron scepter, which is what Jesus is doing in Revelation 19:15.

Many scholars recognize the symbol of the dragon's attack on the child as the literal attack of Herod on the children of Bethlehem in an attempt to take Jesus' life. Spiritual forces nearly always accomplish their purposes through human agency. Here, Satan employed Roman soldiers to try to kill Jesus at birth, and he did it again at Jesus' crucifixion.

Considering the big picture, then, it makes the most sense here to understand the woman who gives birth to Jesus not as Mary, an individual, but as Israel as a nation. Later, in Revelation 17, a woman again represents an entire group of people, so this would be consistent with the way the symbol of a woman seems to be employed in Revelation.

So, using Herod and, later, the Jewish leaders and Roman authorities as his tools, Satan attempts to destroy Jesus, but Jesus is snatched up to God and his throne. He ascends to heaven after his crucifixion. The woman goes out into the desert.

By this time, Jesus and the new Christian church he had formed had become the new Israel, as we discussed earlier. So in later history, the woman still represents the people of God but now in the form of the Christian church rather than the nation of Israel. The symbol remains constant, just as God's people remain constant, though the form in which they exist changes.

After the child is caught up to God and the woman flees to the wilderness, where does the dragon go? It seems as though he goes to heaven along with the child, because in the next scene we see the dragon at war in heaven with Michael.

> And there was war in heaven. Michael and his angels fought against the dragon, and the dragon and his angels fought back. But he was not strong enough, and they lost their place in heaven. The great dragon was hurled down—that ancient serpent called the devil, or Satan, who leads the whole world astray. He was hurled to the earth, and his angels with him.
>
> Then I heard a loud voice in heaven say: "Now have come the salvation and the power and the kingdom of our God, and the authority of his Christ. For the accuser of our brothers, who accuses them before our God day and night, has been hurled down. They overcame him by the blood of the Lamb and by the word of their testimony; they did not love their lives so much as to shrink from death. Therefore rejoice, you heavens and you who dwell in them! But woe to the earth and the sea, because the devil has gone down to you! He is filled with fury, because he knows that his time is short" (Revelation 12:7–12).

Michael and the male child

Notice that Michael is not introduced or explained. So we should suspect that we've met him before in Revelation. The information we have here is that Michael is in heaven battling Satan, and the only character we have already met in Revelation who could be in heaven and who could be fighting Satan is Jesus himself. So Michael, the male child, and Jesus are all different names for the same character.

How can Jesus be an angel?

Many people stall on the idea that Michael and Jesus are the same person, and not without reason. Elsewhere in Scripture, Michael is referred to as an angel. If we believe that Jesus is Michael, does that mean we think Jesus is a created being not quite on the same level with God? No.

The word *angel* as it was understood in John's day is different from what we think of today. We often use the word *angel* to describe a kind of being, while the Old Testament uses the word to describe a function or a job. It's simply a title, if you will. The word *angel* means messenger. If someone brings his own message rather than sending a different messenger, then he is the messenger. He is his own angel, so to speak.

So for Jesus to be called an angel is not to make him any less divine. It doesn't relegate him to the status of a created being. It simply describes what he's doing at a particular moment, which is delivering a message in person as his own messenger.

If you want to confirm this, check out the story of Moses at the burning bush. We all know it was God in the bush speaking to Moses, because no angel ever tells a human to take off his shoes because he's on holy ground. God does tell Moses to do that, but in the story he is also called the angel of the Lord. He was delivering his own message. We don't want to get too far afield on this subject, but it's necessary to briefly address it so that no one gets derailed.

Back to the dragon and Michael

So the dragon follows the male child to heaven and war ensues there. Michael is victorious, the dragon is cast back down to earth, and a loud voice says, "Woe to the earth and the sea because the devil has come down to you" (verse 12).

See the sequence so far? First, there is war in heaven (verses 1–4); then there is war on earth when the dragon attacks the male child and the woman flees to desert (verses 4, 6); the child goes to heaven (verse 5); war ensues in heaven again with Michael (verses 7–9); then finally the war returns to earth again (verses 12–17).

This sequence may raise some questions in your mind, so let's clarify what we mean at each stage. When the rebellion began in heaven, that was the first war between Christ and Satan. It hasn't been revealed to us exactly what war looks like in heaven, but Satan and his followers were cast out of heaven physically at that time—at least as physically as a spirit can be.

At that point, Satan moved his rebellion to earth. The war on earth was physical as well. Satan and his angels attacked Jesus and God's people with physical violence, which culminated in Christ's death on the cross. But Satan couldn't keep Jesus down, and Jesus ascended to heaven again.

The next part of the war in heaven seems to have been more of a spiritual war, if that's a good way to describe it. Evidently, before the cross, Satan still had some access to heaven. The story of Job says that the sons of God came together from around the universe and Satan joined them as the representative and ruler of earth.

After the cross, though, Satan was cast out of heaven for good. In other words, this casting out was final. The war was over. Satan had lost. What happened in the courts of heaven, we can only speculate. But when Jesus was enthroned after his resurrection, perhaps Satan tried to protest and God the Father informed Satan that he must now leave and never return. He had no more access to heaven or other worlds. He was exiled and quarantined to earth. Thus, "Woe to the earth for the devil has gone down to you."

The war was over but it hadn't quite ended. The final effort at rebellion on earth is also more of a spiritual war because it involves deception more than physical violence. And now, since the dragon can no longer directly attack Christ, he attacks the children of the woman, the last-day people of God.

Note that the dragon plays a part in each of the four attacks, which seems strong evidence that this is a sequence of history. The dragon keeps appearing at different and successive times that must happen in sequence.

So with the background of the original war in heaven at the beginning of earth's history, we then see the first stage of Christian history: Jesus' birth, the cross, his ascension, and his enthronement with his Father. This is where Christian history begins.

Gospel interlude

Before we go into stage two of Christian history, we find that a gospel interlude appears in verse 11. John does this frequently. As we see some heavy and frightening events going on, John pauses to remind us who is in control of all things, so we can keep our perspective. *Don't worry about what you're seeing here,* he says. *Remember that we know who wins. God does. Relax.*

So here is this brief reminder of good news: "They overcame him by the blood of the Lamb and by the word of their testimony; they did not love their lives so much as to shrink from death" (Revelation 12:11).

The word *overcome* is one of the most important words in Revelation. You see it in many places, and in nearly every case it refers either to Jesus Christ or to his people. In a few instances it is attributed to the beast power, but those are counterfeit situations, which will show up later.

In this case it refers to God's people, and it says that God's people overcome "by the blood of the Lamb." The Lamb, of course, is the Lamb of God who takes away the sin of the world. This is an obvious reference to Jesus on the cross. It's because of Jesus' death that we have any hope of overcoming.

The question is how does the cross make a difference in overcoming? We understand how it makes a difference in *forgiveness* of sin, because that is how Jesus paid our penalty for us. But how does the cross make a difference in *overcoming* sin? That's like saying someone paid a lot of money to get you out of financial debt but that payment is also able to keep you from wracking up more debt. How can that be?

The cross identifies sin for what it really is

Here are a couple of ways the cross helps us to overcome day by day. First of all, the cross identifies sin in a gut-wrenching way. It seems that Satan has leveled some pretty awful accusations against God and his system of government. He has questioned whether or not God is really a God of love and freedom. And apparently Satan was convincing enough that he managed to fool a third of the population of heaven into believing his lies. These were perfect beings with no sin, and Satan managed to convince them to follow him. Among those who didn't follow him, many questions would have remained in their minds. Could Satan have had a point?

So God in his infinite wisdom allowed Satan to make his case for everyone to see whether evil might be better than love, if rebellion might be better than obedience. The universe must see the end result of Satan's system of government. And the universe saw it at the cross.

If the end result of sin is that it would cruelly crucify the most gentle, kind, loving Being in the universe—who gave himself up to it voluntarily, no less—if sin is capable of doing that, then sin is as hideous as it gets. The cross not only forgives sin, it shows sin for what it really is, underneath its false advertising.

The cross shows what we are worth

Something else the cross does that enables us to overcome is to prove our value. How much sin is the result of undervaluing ourselves? We see it from childhood, the way we put others down in order to build ourselves up, to feel more valuable. We humans kill each other in order prove we are on top. We fight to be first, best, most valuable player. We steal to get the things that make us valuable in other people's eyes.

The underlying cause of sin may well be a misunderstanding of how valuable we actually are. If we understood our true value, we wouldn't spend our lives trying to prove it to ourselves and others.

How valuable are you? If we were boiled down to our chemical components, those who calculate such things say we would be worth about $12 each, give or take a little, depending on your size. But really, we aren't valued in terms of our physical worth; we are valued in terms of the value we have in the eyes of others.

That is a terrible reality if you are looking in the wrong place for your value. However, it is the most incredibly good reality if you are looking to the right place for your value. The fact is that the most valuable Being in the universe valued you so much that he gave up more than we can ever comprehend in order to rescue you from certain death. Why did he do it? Just one reason: because he values you.

Still, we have heard that statement so often that it doesn't have the impact it should have. It would probably do more for our sense of self worth to learn that the president of the United States was coming to visit us to seek our advice on some important decision. That would make us feel pretty valuable. But we've heard about Jesus so much that it doesn't compute that the king of the universe didn't come just to visit you but came to die for you.

How valuable is Jesus?

Our value doesn't compute also because we can't comprehend how valuable Jesus is. How valuable is he? Well, he's the creator of everything, which means he is more valuable than everything. The artist is always more valuable than the art, because if the art is lost, the artist can always make more. If the artist is lost, then all is lost. Jesus, the creator, is more valuable than all of the gold and diamonds in the world combined. He is more valuable than everything on earth combined. He is more valuable than our entire solar system and the entire universe no matter what fabulous riches are contained in it, because he created all of it! How valuable is Jesus? It is no overstatement to say that Jesus is everything.

He valued you so much that he stopped everything he was doing in the eternal heaven and came to this dark, disgusting planet to live a life of pain and to die a cruel death, because he thinks you are valuable. He thinks you are worth it. How valuable does that make you? It makes you as valuable as Jesus himself, because Jesus gave his most valuable life in exchange for yours.

Don't look anywhere else for your value. Don't look to your family; don't look to your job or to your friends. Don't look to who you know or what you have. Look only to Jesus on the cross and realize who he is and why he hung there.

The cross makes it possible for you and me to overcome because the cross removes the need for the very thing that drives us toward sin—a search for our own value.

You are a child of the king of the universe, and he loves you more than any child you have ever loved. He values you more than his own life. He thinks you are the coolest, most awesome friend to have. Understanding that should change the way we see ourselves and the ways we try to show ourselves valuable. The only approval we should be concerned with is his.

Sharing faith helps us overcome

The second way God's people overcome in Revelation 12:11 is by the word of their testimony. What is the word of someone's testimony? It's not really that hard to understand. We still use the term sometimes. *Share your testimony. Share what Jesus has done in your life.* As odd as it may sound, an integral part of overcoming evil is sharing your testimony, being a witness to others of what Christ has done for you and in you.

Expressing your faith to another person always affects your own faith. Intellectual knowledge of the cross is a far different thing than heart knowledge of the cross. Sharing your faith moves head knowledge to heart knowledge—from rational knowledge to a heart's understanding.

Whenever you share your faith, two people are listening: the other person and you. Talk garbage, and we will have more garbage. Talk faith and we will have more faith.

Overcoming includes losing fear of death

The third stage of overcoming in Revelation 12:11 is losing our fear of death. Is it really possible to not fear death?

Back in the 1400s, John Hus, a Christian reformer, got crosswise with the church. He refused to recant his Bible-based beliefs, which the church called heresy, and for his trouble they stood him on a pile of dry wood and paper and tied him to a post in the middle. As they kindled the fire at his feet, among his final words were, "In the truth of the Gospel which I have written, taught, and preached I will die today with gladness." No fear.

"They overcame him by the blood of the Lamb and by the word of their testimony; they did not love their lives so much as to shrink from death."

That sounds like two separate thoughts, but it's one sentence. The result of overcoming by the blood of the Lamb and by the word of our testimony is that we will lose our fear of death. That's how the Christian martyrs were able to stand strong. If death was the only alternative to losing Jesus, then so be it. Life without Jesus was not even an option to be considered.

We can overcome Satan just as Jesus did, but we do it by (1) claiming his blood as our salvation, (2) sharing our faith in him, and (3) staying in that mode of operation until we become more willing to die than to give him up.

That's the gospel interlude in the middle of the sequence of history of Revelation 12. It's a powerful verse.

We have already looked at stage one: the time of Jesus and his disciples (Revelation 12:5, 10–12). Next we'll look at stage two, which is a central period of persecution—the Middle Ages and beyond (Revelation 12:6, 14–16). After that we will look into stage three, which is at the time of the end in Revelation 12:17.

Into the wilderness

The woman fled into the desert to a place prepared for her by God, where she might be taken care of for 1,260 days. . . . The woman was given the two wings of a great eagle, so that she might fly to the place prepared for her in the desert, where she would be taken care of for a time, times and half a time, out of the serpent's reach. Then from his mouth the serpent spewed water like a river, to overtake the woman and sweep her away with the torrent. But the earth helped the woman by opening its mouth and swallowing the river that the dragon had spewed out of his mouth (Revelation 12:6, 14–16).

The story of God's people that began in verse 6 resumes in verse 14. The language is almost the same except that in verse 6 the number is 1,260 days and in verse 14 it says a time, times, and half a time.

The phrase "time, times, and half a time" is unusual and is used nowhere else in the Bible except in Daniel. So right away we know that John is again building on the visions of Daniel in this passage. No surprise there.

This particular span of time is significant because it is mentioned several times in Revelation. Twice it is mentioned as 42 months, which breaks down to 1,260 days by the ancient calendar. So 42 months and 1,260 days are the same time period. However, in both cases that the time is stated as 42 months, it's on the negative side of Revelation's agenda. In Revelation 11:2 it is the time period that the Gentiles trample the holy city, and in Revelation 13:5 it is the time period that the beast makes war against the saints. Both of these are negative things for God's people.

The two instances that the time period is stated as 1,260 days, it is on the positive side of Revelation's agenda—God's side. Revelation 11:3 describes the two witnesses prophesying for 1,260 days. The two witnesses are good guys. And in Revelation 12:6, the woman, representing God's people, is cared for in the desert for 1,260 days.

In Revelation 12:14 the time is stated as a time, times, and half a time, just as in Daniel. The view is widely accepted, based on the language that a "time" is a year, that this phrase is more accurately translated "a time, two times, and half a time," or a year, two years, and half a year, adding up to three and a half years. That much is generally accepted among scholars. Your Bible may even note it in the margin.

However, disagreement arises when some assert that the three and a half years are literal years while others assert they are symbolic years. Considering our previous discussion about symbolism as the default mode for Revelation, we should begin at that point. Any time we feel the need to switch from symbolic to literal, we must build a solid case for doing so. If we can't build that case then we know we must work in default mode, which is symbolism. No one has yet been able to build a strong enough case for switching to literal time in this instance. Also, it seems a little too coincidental that three and a half years just happens to be 42 months or 1,260 days, by the standard prophetic calendar. That would seem to be a far-fetched coincidence.

What strengthens this idea more is the description of the beast in Revelation 13 and the little horn power in Daniel 7. The little horn power blasphemes against God and makes war against the saints for a time, times and half a time. In Revelation 13 the beast is blaspheming God and making war against the saints for 42 months. Knowing the way prophecy uses different symbols to describe the same characters, we already have good reason to suspect that the little horn power of Daniel 7 and the beast of Revelation 13 may be describing the same power and the same time frame.

It seems pretty solid, then, that 42 months, 1,260 days, and a time, times, and half a time all refer to the same time period, which also fits well into the overall plot of Revelation. There is too much evidence to ignore.

This is important because we gain some valuable clues from these time span texts that we are going to need as we move into the next chapter of Revelation.

First, we see from Revelation 11:3 that the two witnesses are living in obscurity during this 1,260 day time period. Most people agree that the two witnesses are good guys and that they probably symbolize the Bible—the Old and New Testaments, the Law and the Prophets. Many commentators still refer to the Bible as "the witnesses." During the 1,260-day period, the two witnesses are living in obscurity. They are out of sight for the most part. This is one valuable clue.

We gain another clue from the 42-month time period in Revelation 13:5, where we see that the saints are persecuted by a great power. When we combine these clues with the prophecies of Daniel, we begin to see that this great power arises out of the long-term kingdoms that Daniel saw in his visions. That leads to a critically important realization: the 1,260 days and 42 months and three and a half years cannot be literal time periods. The evidence calls for a much greater span of time. Some interpretations of Revelation attempt to work within the boundaries of a literal 1,260 days, but in the grand plot of Revelation those interpretations don't hold up in the long run.

Understanding the reality of the length of these time periods is crucial because it will help lead us to the identification of other symbols in Revelation, including the beast of Revelation 13. Now we need to explore the day-for-a-year principle.

Day for a year

I was preparing to preach somewhere in Russia once, and I asked my translator how long I should plan to speak. He relayed my question to the pastor, and the reply came back, "One hour." Then the pastor said something else, and my translator laughed and said, "Not prophetic time!" I laughed as well, because I knew what he was talking about.

He was referring to what is often called the prophetic "day-for-a-year" principle. When prophecy talks about a day, it means a year. The Bible doesn't explicitly state this principle, but as we saw before, the Bible doesn't explicitly state a lot of things. The Bible does provide general guiding principles that make clear the way we should understand a specific question.

We can start with the Bible to show first that the Hebrews had a mindset that understood the day-for-a-year principle. They called it a sabbatical year, or weeks of days and weeks of years, a seven-year cycle corresponding to the seven-day cycle in which the seventh year was a year of rest for the land, just as the seventh day is a day of rest for the week. Leviticus 26 and 2 Chronicles 36 both define this sabbatical year.

Here are a few examples of how Israel worked within this day-for-a year principle. After God brought Israel out of slavery in Egypt, Numbers 14:34 tells us, he took them to the border of the land he had promised them. They were to go in and conquer this land. However, the spies they sent to explore came back after 40 days with a bad report, saying, "We can't conquer this land." So God said, "Just as you wish. You will never see Canaan. In 40 years your children will go instead." God sentenced Israel to 40 years of wandering in the wilderness, one year for each day that the spies explored Canaan. This sentence made sense to them in spite of the fact that they didn't like it.

Another example of this kind of numbering is found in Ezekiel 4:4–6, where God tells Ezekiel to lie on his side for 390 days, a day for each year of Israel's rebellion.

We find some examples outside of the Bible during the same period of history. Archaeologists have discovered how Hammurabi, an ancient Near Eastern ruler, declared a 30-day celebration, one day for each year of his reign. The Jews at Qumran used the same principle, taking seven-year periods and calling them weeks.

Finally, a clincher appears in Daniel 9 with a 70-week prophecy (490 days) that takes us from Persia in the sixth century BC all the way to the time of Christ, 490 years later. The prophecy said 490 days, but the span was 490 years. Interestingly, all scholars accept the day-for-a-year principle in the 70-week prophecy because they can't get from the sixth century BC to the coming of the Messiah in 70 literal weeks of days.

One gets the feeling that someone is trying to defend a specific agenda when they will accept the day-for-a-year principle in one place because the evidence requires it and not in another place even though the evidence requires it. In the grand scheme of prophecy, the day-for-a-year principle makes sense.

When to use a day for a year

When do we to apply the day-for-a-year principle? When it's convenient? Only when we want to? We should be pretty uncomfortable with that idea. We should consider applying the day-for-a-year principle in two situations. First, when we run into unusual numbers, and second, when the time span requires it.

When my son reached three and a half years of age, I couldn't resist a little pastor-style humor and started telling people my son was 42 months old, or 1,260 days old, or better yet, that he was a time, times, and half a time years old. The normal way to state the time span is three and a half years. To state it as 42 months, 1,260 days, or time, times, and half a time is to put it in an unusual way. So numbers that seem unusual seem good candidates for being symbolic.

The second situation, using the day-for-a-year principle when the time spans seem to require it, comes up when it's necessary to account for long-range prophecies and long-term kingdoms.

In Daniel's prophecies, he sees four animals. Each of these animals represents a kingdom that was to come.

- The first was Babylon, the lion, which ruled for 66 years.
- Then came Medo-Persia, the bear, which ruled for 207 years.
- Then came Greece, the leopard, which ruled for 163 years.

• Finally came Rome, a horrifying creature (the biggest, strongest, cruelest kingdom), which ruled for well over 500 years.

The total is about a thousand years' worth of kingdoms ruling the earth.

Out of that last kingdom comes the mysterious and powerful little horn, speaking great things against God. The beast itself was fearful enough, but Daniel focuses on this little horn, because to him that is the truly terrifying part. And this little-horn power rules for a time, times, and half a time.

Considering the huge time span covered by the four kingdoms and all of the horrific things that happened to God's people during that time at the hands of those powers, does it make sense that the most terrifying little horn only reigns for three and a half literal years? No power could in three and a half literal years even begin to act more terrible toward God's people than the other cruel powers that had conducted a thousand years of persecution. If you're in doubt about the length and intensity of the little horn's persecution, just read a few pages of *Foxe's Book of Martyrs*. The persecuting powers of the little horn made a science of inventing terrible tortures for Christians. A literal 1,260 days simply doesn't make sense in the overall story, while 1,260 years makes perfect sense.

Since the time period is mentioned in an unusual way and a literal interpretation of the three and a half years doesn't make sense to the story, we realize that we should test it out by studying more deeply. Eventually we discover that in Daniel's vision, this little horn power actually bridges the entire time from ancient Rome to the time of the end. If that's the case, the prophecy requires 1,260 years to be fulfilled.

Stage two: continued

Let's go on to the second stage of Christian history in Revelation 12:15–16. The woman has been in the wilderness for 1,260 prophetic days, which we now know to be 1,260 years. "Then from his mouth the serpent spewed water like a river, to overtake the woman and sweep her away with the torrent. But the earth helped the woman by opening its mouth and swallowing the river that the dragon had spewed out of his mouth."

So during these 1,260 years, after the fall of pagan Rome and during the Middle Ages, this is what the dragon or the serpent was up to. He was spewing water out of his mouth—symbolically speaking.

We know a lot of persecution was happening during the Middle Ages, which could explain the symbol of the serpent attacking God's people with this river of water. But the allusion here shows us there's more going on than that. Many Bibles have a cross-reference in the margin pointing to Genesis 3:1. It is a strong allusion to the story of the serpent in the Garden of Eden deceiving Eve. He's telling her lies. At this point Revelation clearly intends for us to recall that story in order to interpret its meaning.

Throughout history, Satan has indeed persecuted God's people through the different pagan kingdoms up through the Roman Empire, and then, I'm ashamed to admit, through the Christian church during the Middle Ages. However, persecution isn't the only way Satan works. He uses deception also. Jesus called him the father of lies for good reason. He is a master illusionist, a great deceiver. When it comes to determining what he is up to, you cannot trust what you see and hear. Satan is better at deception than every magician or illusionist on earth combined. If that doesn't give us cause for pause, it should.

Remember Jesus' disturbing words concerning the end of time in Matthew 24:24? "False Christs and false prophets will appear and perform great signs and miracles to deceive even the elect —if that were possible." This is where we are headed. By the time we're done, we will begin to see the frightening nature of the final great deception that the serpent has in store.

In Genesis the serpent sent deception and persecution to try to destroy the woman, God's people. During the Middle Ages, under the tyrannical rule of the Christian church, persecution of God's people included torture, burning at the stake, and so on. Unfortunately, we know too well what persecution looks like in Christian history, but what does deception look like in Christian history? Wouldn't it be false doctrine, false religion, misrepresenting God? What else could possibly fit the bill for deceiving God's people?

Satan deceived perfect heavenly angels concerning what they believed about God. Satan deceived Eve concerning what she believed about God. Satan continues to deceive people in exactly the same way today. Knowing that people are drawn to religion, Satan knows he must turn people away from true religion where they actually find God, so he introduces false religion where they will not find God.

Earth to the rescue

Revelation 12:16 says that the earth helped the woman. Earth is one of the symbols in Revelation that is a positive force in one place and a negative force in another place. Here the earth helps the people of God by swallowing the river that is coming to destroy them. If the river is persecution and deception is false religion, then the earth must be something that provides for God's people a place of refuge away from persecution and false religion. So here the earth is a positive symbol. Elsewhere in Revelation, earth becomes a negative symbol.

We also detect in Revelation 12:15–16 an allusion to Israel's Exodus. "You stretched out your right hand and the earth swallowed them" (Exodus 15:12). This is the song of Moses and Israel after their miraculous deliverance from the Red Sea. Referring to the Egyptian army, Israel sang to God, "You stretched out your right hand and the earth swallowed them." In the symbol in Revelation, just as in the Exodus, God provided for his people a place of refuge. For 1,260 years of terrible times for God's people during the Middle Ages, when persecution and false Christianity threatened to destroy them, God provided safety and preservation, first of all in the Alps in Europe and eventually in the New World, here in our religiously free United States.

These are the first two stages of Christian history in Revelation 12. Stage one was the time of Jesus and his apostles, when the Christian church began. Stage two was the Middle Ages, when Satan used the Christian church for 1,260 years to persecute and deceive God's faithful people. These two stages are now behind us. Next, we move toward stage three—the final conflict.

Stage three: the final conflict

"Then the dragon was enraged at the woman and went off to make war against the rest of her offspring—those who obey God's commandments and hold to the testimony of Jesus" (Revelation 12:17).

This, as we will see, is the final crisis of earth's history. The dragon is enraged because he has repeatedly failed. First, the male child escaped him (verse 5); he wasn't strong enough to win the war in heaven (verses 7–9); and the woman escapes him into the desert (verses 6, 14). So this is the end for him. This is his last chance, and he knows it. Every time he has made a frontal assault upon God, he has failed. So he goes away from battling God, where he is always losing, to make war against the children of the woman who had escaped him. The children of the woman are described as those who keep the commandments of God and have the testimony of Jesus—God's last-day people.

The battle lines are drawn clearly: the dragon versus God's last-day people in a final great battle. He is making war. But the dragon does not make a frontal assault this time. He goes to the beach in search of allies who will help him.

Revelation 12:17 sets the stage for the battle that Revelation 13 and 14 are going to flesh out. The battle has two sides. The dragon's side will be explained in chapter 13, and the side of God and his people will be explained in chapter 14.

Study Guide Outline

Chapter 9

1. Revelation 12 is a prophetic overview of _____ history.

2. Each time a new character is introduced in Revelation, John takes a moment to _____ that character.

3. If what seems like a new character appears in the story but without a _____, we have probably seen this character before under a different name or symbol.

4. It seems as though Revelation has many _____, but there are only a few characters represented by different names and symbols.

5. The woman of Revelation 12 represents the _____ of God in some form.

6. The red dragon is _____. The male child is _____.

7. Michael in Revelation 12 has to be _____, and this does not mean that he is a created angel.

8. The three stages of Christian history are:

   a. Stage one: The time of _____ and the apostles (Revelation 12:5, 10–12).

   b. Stage two: The time of the _____ _____ and beyond (Revelation 12:6, 14–16).

   c. Stage three: The time of earth's final _____ (Revelation 12:17).

9. The 42 _____, 1,260 _____, and a time, times, and half a time all refer to the same time period.

10. The day-for-a-year principle should be considered for _____ numbers and when the situation requires it.

11. The serpent spewing water out of his mouth is an allusion to the serpent _____ Eve in Genesis 3.

12. Satan attacks God's people through persecution and _____.

13. The children of the woman are God's _____ people.

14. Revelation 12:17 sets the stage for the final _____ of earth's history.

The Dragon's War

Revelation 13

Are you on pins and needles over this chapter? You should be, but not just because we're going to find a whole bunch of clues that will help us to identify some nasty beasts. Remember what the purpose of prophecy is and is not? It isn't to satisfy our curiosity about the future; it's supposed to give us just enough of an idea about the future that we can pattern our lives correctly today in regard to the future.

Therefore, one of the primary things we need is an understanding of the entire plot of the story of Revelation. We won't be primarily attempting to identify the symbols. We will concentrate on seeing the story itself first. Once we know the story, we will be able to identify the symbols more accurately.

We've just seen three stages in Christian history, and we will see stages two and three covered again in Revelation 13. Remember that Revelation 12:17 sets the stage for what we'll be seeing in chapter 13.

The dragon was enraged with the woman and went away from attacking God and the woman to attack her children, God's end-time people—those who keep the commandments and have the testimony of Jesus. That verse was stage three, the last stage of Christian history, which is the final great battle at the time of the end. Two clearly marked sides participate: the dragon's side and the side of God's people. Revelation 12:17 and Revelation 13 outline this conflict by employing a literary device we call the backflash.

In movies and books we often see the story start off with a battle scene or some other high drama designed to draw us in. Then the story flashes back in time to give us some history of the character or a past situation that helps us understand what we saw in the opening scene. Something similar is happening in the last verse of Revelation 12 and in Revelation 13.

Revelation 12:17 begins with a peek at the final great battle. That gives us the context. But then we need to be introduced to the characters involved and learn their history. Parts of Revelation 13 give us that history before cutting back to the final battle in order to explain the actions of those characters in the conflict.

Here's how it works, using the beast from the sea as the first example. At the time of the final conflict (stage three of Christian history), the dragon stands on the shore of the sea, and as John watches, a creature comes up out of the sea. This is a new character, so Revelation pauses the final battle scene to describe the physical attributes of this new beast character and some of its history (verses 1–7).

The history of this beast as described in Revelation 13:1–7 comes from the second stage of Christian history, the Middle Ages. (This beast has been in operation for a long time before its actions during the end times.) Once the introduction is complete, Revelation returns to the final battle in verses 12–18 to show the actions of the beast from the sea at that time. Later, Revelation does the same thing with the beast from the land, using a backflash in verse 11 and then flashing forward to the final conflict in verses 12–18.

This isn't just made up to fit what we are reading. The structure of Revelation 13 is supported by the grammar. If you happen to be good at Greek grammar, you will note that the introduction of the sea beast in verses 1–7 is written in the *aorist* tense, which means it is action in the past.

Let's use an illustration to help us understand the tenses in Revelation 13. Suppose your friend is planning to skydive next week, and he's so absorbed in it that he dreams about it. When he wakes up he tells you, "I had a dream. I jumped out of an airplane and parachuted to earth!" Jumped? Parachuted? Those are past tense statements. And yet the event is still in the future. He describes the experience in the past tense because in his dream he was located in the future, and he was telling what happened from that perspective.

The same thing happens in Revelation 13. John was living in the time of stage one of Christian history—the time of Jesus and the apostles. However, in vision John is located in the time of the final battle, stage three of Christian history—in the future. So when he speaks of stage two of Christian history, which for him is still in the future, he speaks in past tense of the things that were yet to happen.

The Greek grammar of Revelation 12:17 is written in present and future tense and covers the time of the final battle. Revelation 13:1–7 concerning the Middle Ages is written in past tense. Verses 8–10 are written in the present and future tense at the time of the final conflict. Then verse 11, which introduces the land beast, flashes back to the *aorist* tense, action in past time, to introduce the history of the land beast before the final battle. Verses 12–18 flash back, using the present and future tense, to describe the actions of the two beasts during the final battle. These shifts are clear in the original Greek, but we can't see it as well in the English.

The following sections outline the entire text of Revelation 13, along with some added information (in boldface) as though John were clarifying each section for us. Come back to this outline if the sequence becomes confusing later on.

At the time of the final battle I saw . . .

"The dragon was enraged at the woman and went off to make war against the rest of her offspring—those who obey God's commandments and hold to the testimony of Jesus" (Rev. 12:17).

"And the dragon stood on the shore of the sea" (Rev. 13:1).

Switching to a time before the final battle, I saw some background information about the pedigree and history of a new character I had not seen before . . .

"And I saw a beast coming out of the sea. He had ten horns and seven heads, with ten crowns on his horns, and on each head a blasphemous name. The beast I saw resembled a leopard, but had feet like those of a bear and a mouth like that of a lion. The dragon gave the beast his power and his throne and great authority. One of the heads of the beast seemed to have had a fatal wound, but the fatal wound had been healed. The whole world was astonished and followed the beast. Men worshiped the dragon because he had given authority to the beast, and they also worshiped the beast and asked, 'Who is like the beast? Who can make war against him?' " (Rev. 13:1–4).

"The beast was given a mouth to utter proud words and blasphemies and to exercise his authority for forty-two months. He opened his mouth to blaspheme God, and to slander his name and his dwelling place and those who live in heaven. He was given power to make war against the saints and to conquer them. And he was given authority over every tribe, people, language and nation" (Rev. 13:5–7).

Switching back to the time of the final battle, I saw how this beast was involved in the battle . . .

"All inhabitants of the earth will worship the beast—all whose names have not been written in the book of life belonging to the Lamb that was slain from the creation of the world.

"He who has an ear, let him hear. If anyone is to go into captivity, into captivity he will go. If anyone is to be killed with the sword, with the sword he will be killed. This calls for patient endurance and faithfulness on the part of the saints" (Rev. 13:8–9).

Switching to a time before the final battle, I saw some background information on a new character I had not seen before . . .

"Then I saw another beast, coming out of the earth. He had two horns like a lamb, but he spoke like a dragon" (Rev. 13:11).

Switching back to the time of the final battle, I saw the ways both of these characters would be involved in the battle . . .

"He exercised all the authority of the first beast on his behalf, and made the earth and its inhabitants worship the first beast, whose fatal wound had been healed. And he performed great and miraculous signs, even causing fire to come down from heaven to earth in full view of men. Because of the signs he was given power to do on behalf of the first beast, he deceived the inhabitants of the earth. He ordered them to set up an image in honor of the beast who was wounded by the sword and yet lived. He was given power to give breath to the image of the first beast, so that it could speak and cause all who refused to worship the image to be killed. He also forced everyone, small and great, rich and poor, free and slave, to receive a mark on his right hand or on his forehead, so that no one could buy or sell unless he had the mark, which is the name of the beast or the number of his name.

"This calls for wisdom. If anyone has insight, let him calculate the number of the beast, for it is man's number. His number is 666" (Rev. 13:12–18).

The beast from the sea

"And I saw a beast coming out of the sea. He had ten horns and seven heads, with ten crowns on his horns, and on each head a blasphemous name. The beast I saw resembled a leopard, but had feet like those of a bear and a mouth like that of a lion" (Rev. 13:1–2).

This description ought to bring two things to our minds immediately. First, this beast from the sea resembles the dragon in Revelation 12. Both have seven heads and 10 horns. Second, this beast resembles the four animals in Daniel's vision: a lion, a bear, a leopard with four heads, and a ten-horned beast.

The beast coming out of the sea in Revelation 13 looked like a leopard, had the feet of a bear, the mouth of a lion, some of the characteristics of the little horn, and seven heads. None of the animals in Daniel's vision had seven heads, but all of them together total seven. The sea beast of Revelation 13 is an obvious composite of all of the beasts of Daniel 7 that represented the world empires of Babylon, Medo-Persia, Greece, and Rome. We don't have to figure those out because those interpretations are provided in the text.

The beast coming out of the sea is a combination of all these beasts and the dragon. The beast rose to power out of, and after, the four kingdoms, so it has a prophetic history of pagan political power in its past. But as this sea beast rises to power after and out of the Roman Empire, it takes on a new face.

Reading on, we see that in the Middle Ages this sea beast blasphemed, which is a religious action. Jesus was accused of blasphemy because he claimed to be the Son of God. Blasphemy means to equate yourself with God, which evidently this beast from the sea is doing. So it is more than just a political power; it's also a religious power.

Counterfeit

"One of the heads of the beast seemed to have had a fatal wound, but the fatal wound had been healed. The whole world was astonished and followed the beast" (Rev. 13:3).

By now you can see that the little horn of Daniel and the sea beast of Revelation represent the same power. One of the sea beast's heads was killed and his fatal wound had been healed, just like the little horn of Daniel. The Greek wording makes it clear that this was a wound that killed, so something died and then came back to life—a resurrection. That makes us think of Jesus Christ, the one most famous for having died and risen again. But this beast is not Jesus Christ. It is a power working with the dragon, the enemy of Jesus Christ.

Satan is putting together a major deception that could, if possible, deceive even the elect, the true believers. We don't have enough evidence to say this conclusively just yet, but we could be seeing a counterfeit to Jesus' death and resurrection as part of a great deception to come.

Normally conspiracy theories don't hold up to scrutiny. Human beings aren't really capable of putting together some of the complicated conspiracies that become urban legend and movies. However, we are not dealing with human beings here. We're dealing with an enemy who has already shown himself exceptionally capable of grand conspiracy against God for thousands of years. So for once we are not closed to the possibility of a major conspiracy. Indeed, we're warned to look for one. Still, the skeptic in us doesn't want to see a conspiracy where there isn't one. So let's look at where this suspicion might lead in the text.

Slaughtered

The word *sphazo* that the NIV translates "fatal wound" is a significant phrase in the Greek language; it means literally "slaughtered to death." Greek has several words that describe killing, and this one is used infrequently. You find it mostly in the context of the killing of the sanctuary lamb.

In Revelation 13 the same word, *sphazo,* is used in verse three for the sea beast and in verse eight for Jesus. "One of the heads of the beast seemed to have had a *fatal wound,* but the fatal wound had been healed" (Revelation 13:3). "All inhabitants of the earth will worship the beast—all whose names have not been written in the book of life belonging to the *Lamb that was slain* from the creation of the world" (verse 8).

Given the uniqueness of the word *sphazo* and the fact that it is nearly always used in connection with the slain lamb of the Old Testament sanctuary, it seems obvious that Revelation intends a connection between the slain lamb and the wounded beast. This is another allusion in the language of Revelation that would have made a clear point to the New Testament Christians with their deep Old Testament background. Revelation clearly intends to communicate the idea that this death and resurrection of the sea beast should be understood as a parallel to the death and resurrection of Christ.

Keep in mind that the dragon is working on a strategy based on deception rather than a frontal assault. Already we have good reason to suspect that he is positioning himself here for an incredibly evil counterfeit.

Pocket that thought because you will need it, and let's keep going with the fatal wound.

We've already established that this beast is a religious power with the pedigree of political power in its history. It arose out of the Roman Empire and is a religious system that gained enough power to wage a massive war on the saints. And after ruling for 1,260 years, this power received a fatal wound. It was "slaughtered to death." We're obviously not dealing with an individual or a standard political kingdom, so what would the death of such a thing look like? It must cease to exist, at least for all practical purposes, as a system or institution. Perhaps it would enter a time of obscurity before being resurrected. This is what happens to the two witnesses of Revelation 11, which is a parallel situation.

Just to illustrate, Apple Computer, when it first came on the scene, was quickly the most popular personal computer. However, Apple Computer "died" for many years. The DOS operating system and, later, Windows took over the market, and Apple entered a period of obscurity. It was for all practical purposes a non-entity except for a few loyal believers. Finally, however, beginning with the iPod, Apple Computer was resurrected and has become a powerful player in the personal computer industry.

Not very long ago the company reported the highest profits of any company in the United States including the oil companies, which always held the top spot in previous years. This illustrates how an organization can die and be resurrected. Now, don't go saying that this proves that Apple Computer is the beast of Revelation 13! It hasn't been a powerful organization for 60 years, much less 1,260. Neither is it a political or spiritual institution. So it's disqualified on many accounts.

It appears more and more likely that we are seeing a counterfeit death and resurrection that parallels Jesus' death and resurrection. Does that mean the beast is a comprehensive counterfeit of Jesus Christ?

Consider this. The dragon and the beast look a lot alike, with seven heads and ten horns. Jesus is also a lot like the Father. He said, "Anyone who has seen me has seen the Father" (John 14:9).

In Matthew 28 he says, "All authority in heaven and on earth has been given to me" (18). That authority came from God the Father. Note where the sea beast's power comes from. Revelation 13:2 says the dragon gives the sea beast "his power and his throne and great authority."

We are seeing here a dragon, which we already know is Satan, who has positioned himself to be a counterfeit of God the Father, while the sea beast is a different counterfeit. Whatever this sea beast is, one thing is becoming frighteningly clear: it's a counterfeit of Jesus Christ.

The sea beast is constantly being described in parallel terms to Jesus Christ. In verse 4 the question is asked, "Who is like the beast?" In Revelation 12 we saw Michael, whose name means, "Who is like God." In some way this beast is attempting to take up the role that Jesus is supposed to have.

Now watch this. The sea beast has a ministry, a time in which it acts, which is 42 months. Jesus' ministry was also 42 months or three and a half years. This time period isn't just a random time. It deliberately parallels Jesus' ministry.

Many scholars have noted how often in Revelation that the good characters and the evil characters look a lot alike.

Whatever we do with the end-time battle, deception is undoubtedly going to play a major role. Is Jesus' warning in Matthew 24:24 starting to take on a whole new meaning? "For false Christs and false prophets will appear doing great signs and wonders that could deceive even the elect if that were possible." Keep this passage in the back of your mind from here on out because we will keep coming back to it.

We're only getting started. Let's move on.

Characteristics of the beast

So far we have seen five stages in the life of this beast: (1) its ancestry; (2) its rise to power; (3) its time of rule; (4) its period of obscurity; (5) its second rise to power as an ally to the dragon at the end of time.

This beast has a political agenda and a religious agenda, blaspheming God, warring against the saints, and slandering God's dwelling place. "He opened his mouth to blaspheme God, and to slander his name and his dwelling place and those who live in heaven. He was given power to make war against the saints and to conquer them. And he was given authority over every tribe, people, language and nation" (Revelation 13:6–7). This is another allusion to the little horn of Daniel. The little horn blasphemes and goes after the saints, attacking the sanctuary, and so on. Revelation connects the actions of the sea beast and the little horn. It's a structural parallel—the strongest kind of parallel.

One of the parallels between the little horn and the sea beast is that both have a time of obscurity following a fatal wound. If we want to identify this beast in history we must look for a power that played a worldwide religious and political role for more than a thousand years but went into obscurity and no longer played that role. Also, it must have the potential to be resurrected for major action just before the end of time.

We know that as a religious power, the sea beast persecuted the people of God. So as we try to identify this power, it must have a history of persecution. Note what the dragon gives the beast. "All authority was given to him over every tribe, nation, language and people." We find the same four words in Revelation 14:6, which is a description of God's last-day people. "Then I saw another angel flying in midair, and he had the eternal gospel to proclaim to those who live on the earth—to every nation, tribe, language and people." This is the third angel's message, the message that God's people are to carry to the world. It is the gospel, the mystery of God that we talked about earlier.

In Revelation 16:13–14, three evil spirits appear, demons that look like frogs coming out of the mouths of the dragon, the beast, and the false prophet (another name for the land beast we are going to discuss next). The three evil spirits are three angels—fallen angels. These three evil angels go out to deceive the nations of the world, just as the three good angels are going out with good news Revelation 14. Both sets of angels deliver a gospel message, one true and the other a counterfeit. The counterfeit to the work of Jesus appears to be a Christian message, but it's a false one.

The beast from the land

Let's leave the sea beast for a while and move on to the third character. The clues just keep coming. "Then I saw another beast, coming out of the earth. He had two horns like a lamb, but he spoke like a dragon" (Revelation 13:11).

First, this beast doesn't have the ancient history that the sea beast has. The land beast's history is described in a single verse, suggesting a power that's relatively new in comparison. In trying to identify him, we don't have any reason to search for some ancient power the way we do for the sea beast.

In the book of Revelation, the sea that the first beast comes from is always negative. The next beast comes out of the earth, and in Revelation, earth is sometimes positive. Remember that the earth swallowed up the river that the dragon had spewed out of its mouth. So the fact that this beast comes out of the land may mean that it at least begins as something good. Add to that the land beast's horns "like a lamb." Lamb-like qualities in Revelation are also good, because the lamb represents Jesus Christ. So far, two positive qualities are assigned to the beast from the land.

The lamb-like horns may indicate a religious side to the beast from the land as well. Consider this: the word *lamb* is mentioned 29 times in Revelation. All but one of them refers to Jesus. The 29th time refers to the land beast. Relatively speaking, the beast that arises out of the earth seems to be more positive than the dragon and the sea beast.

Unfortunately, the beast that looks like a lamb begins at some point to speak like a dragon. At the time of the final battle, he has become one of the bad guys. He looks positive initially, but in the end he supports the dragon.

So now we have three bad guys: the dragon, the sea beast, and the land beast. In the dragon and the sea beast we have a counterfeit of God the Father and God the Son, so what could a third party mean? Should we begin suspecting a counterfeit trinity?

Actions of land beast in the final crisis

Look at Revelation 13:12 and notice that we have moved back to the time of the final battle. We have finished with the backflash for the identification and history of the land beast, and now we're moving back to the view of the final battle. "He exercised all the authority of the first beast on his behalf, and made the earth and its inhabitants worship the first beast, whose fatal wound had been healed" (Revelation 13:12).

During the final crisis this beast from the land will exercise the authority that the sea beast gave to it. What does it do with that authority? It forces everyone on earth to worship the first beast, the one with the fatal wound that was resurrected.[9]

Could we now be seeing an echo of the Holy Spirit's work? What is the role of the Holy Spirit? According to John 15:26, his role is to point people to Jesus. In a disturbing parallel, the land beast points the earth toward the sea beast, the counterfeit of Jesus. Note also that the land beast is

---

9. Notice who has the spotlight: it is the land beast front and center, not the sea beast. If the news is running a story about this, the one on camera is not the sea beast but the land beast. The sea beast is behind the scenes, and his wishes are being carried out by the land beast.

described as "another" beast. Jesus said to his disciples that he would send "another" comforter—the Holy Spirit.

This land beast brings fire down from heaven. "And he performed great and miraculous signs, even causing fire to come down from heaven to earth in full view of men" (Revelation 13:13). The Holy Spirit did the same thing on the Day of Pentecost. Tongues of fire came down upon the apostles, according to Acts 1, when the Holy Spirit came to them in power.

Many Bibles also make a cross-reference to 1 Kings 18:38. Scholars recognize the strong allusion in Revelation to Elijah's Mt. Carmel experience. That was a contest between two gods for the devotion and worship of the people. Elijah and the prophets of Baal are in the spotlight. The term they agreed on was that the god who answers by sending fire from heaven is the true God. This is exactly the same scenario we find in Revelation. The Mt. Carmel experience will be repeated in some fashion, but this time the land beast has the power to cause fire to fall on the wrong altar, thereby convincing the earth to worship the sea beast as the true God.

The land beast creates an image and breathes into him the breath of life. "Because of the signs he was given power to do on behalf of the first beast, he deceived the inhabitants of the earth. He ordered them to set up an image in honor of the beast who was wounded by the sword and yet lived. He was given power to give breath to the image of the first beast, so that it could speak and cause all who refused to worship the image to be killed" (Revelation 13:14–15). The Greek word for spirit is *pneuma*, which means literally "breath," so the parallel between the false and true spirit holds here too.

We're seeing a pattern that amounts to a diabolical deception. A superbly veiled counterfeit trinity is materializing: the dragon as the Father, the sea beast as the Son, and the land beast as the Holy Spirit. By the time we are done, we will see how this unholy trinity even counterfeits the Ten Commandments.

This deception is designed to cause the earth to worship the wrong god—the beast that was resurrected after receiving its fatal wound. The sea beast that already has a long history of spiritual coercion and domination returns for the final battle, and this time it has a supporter that works on its behalf, the land beast.

The image to the beast

The land beast deceives the inhabitants of earth into worshiping the sea beast, and then it instructs the now-convinced people to make an image to the beast they are worshiping. "He was given power to give breath to the image of the first beast, so that it could speak and cause all who refused to worship the image to be killed" (Revelation 13:15).

This is a verse full of information about the nature of the land beast. We have already seen how he brings fire down from heaven, and we saw before how the dragon spewing out water alludes to the serpent's deception in the Garden of Eden. Now we see another allusion to the Garden of Eden. Genesis 2:7 tells us that man was created in the image of God. God gave breath to man, and he became a living soul. In Revelation, the land beast creates an image of the sea beast, breathes life into it, and causes it to speak. A creative act! The counterfeit is obvious.

This land beast, then, causes everyone who won't worship the image to be killed. A few Old Testament stories have remarkable similarities to this scene. In Daniel 3, Nebuchadnezzar set up an image and ordered that everyone worship his image or be killed. Daniel 6 tells the story of everyone being forced to worship King Darius or be thrown to the lions.

Please note: *the primary issue in the final conflict of earth's history is worship.* Those who do not comply with the system of worship established by this unholy trinity will face the death penalty.

The mark of the beast

The mark of the beast is the passage that Revelation students are usually waiting for. Let's deal with it as we did the rest of Revelation, by pulling out our interpretation tools.

"He also forced everyone, small and great, rich and poor, free and slave, to receive a mark on his right hand or on his forehead, so that no one could buy or sell unless he had the mark, which is the name of the beast or the number of his name" (Revelation 13:16–17).

First we look for allusions to see if we can find a broader picture to which Revelation may be pointing. Sure enough, there is an allusion to Ezekiel 9. However, these verses have an even stronger allusion to Deuteronomy 6, where God commands that the Ten Commandments are to be worn on the forehead and on the hand or the wrist.

Opposites in Revelation look remarkably similar—that's what makes a good counterfeit. This mark given by the beast is parallel to the seal of God in Revelation 7 and 14. The mark of the beast, whatever it is, is a counterfeit of the seal of God. Keep that in mind for Revelation 14, when we explore this is more detail.

You recall that the default mode in Revelation is symbolism, and unless we can establish a solid case for interpreting this mark as a literal mark, which we can't, then we should assume it's a symbolic mark. Therefore, we can rule out literal marks such as UPC codes or tattoos, or whatever other kinds of literal marks we may have imagined.

In light of the facts that the central issue in the final conflict is worship; that there is a massive deception going on; and the mark of the beast is in contrast to the seal of God, we can be fairly certain that whatever this mark might be, it is a sign of loyalty to the beast, while the seal of God is a sign of loyalty to God. It need not be a literal mark for someone to display loyalty. There are other ways to accomplish a display of loyalty or disloyalty—such as with obedience or disobedience, for example.

Those who follow the beast fall into two categories: those who are symbolically marked on the forehead and those symbolically marked on the hand. If the mark represents loyalty, it seems likely that those marked on the forehead are those who believe that the counterfeit is genuine. They choose to be loyal to the beast because they are convinced in their minds that he is right and true. They see the fire come down from heaven and are convinced that Jesus has come to earth in some other manner than the noisy way he says he is going to arrive.[10] Many will see the deception of the false trinity and will choose to believe their eyes rather than trust in what the Word of God says. They are symbolically marked on their foreheads.

Others will be marked on the hand. These seem to be the people who, regardless of their convictions, will do whatever it takes to protect themselves. The penalty for not worshiping the image is economic sanctions (no buying or selling) and death. A mark on the hand is likely a symbolic indication that they go along to get along. They do whatever they have to do in order to keep their life, their job, retirement, and so on. They go along with the counterfeit not because they believe it is the truth but to keep their advantages in life.

The number 666

"This calls for wisdom. If anyone has insight, let him calculate the

10. First Thessalonians 4 says Jesus will come in the clouds with a loud trumpet call and a shout of the archangel, and that graves will be thrown open so that every eye will see him at once. He will be making a grand entrance.

number of the beast, for it is man's number. His number is 666" (Revelation 13:18). Everyone is interested in this text, which is odd when you think about it. This is only one small detail in the prophecy, and yet we assign it an unbalanced amount of significance.

We often automatically assume that the number 666 is the mark of the beast, but the text does not say that. It could indicate the mark, but not necessarily. Verse 17 speaks of the mark, and verse 18 speaks of the number of the beast. The way this is worded, the texts can easily point to two separate things—two different clues to the identity of the beast and his purposes.

We do know from the text that this is the number of a man, but we're unsure if it means a specific man or if it is the number of sinful mankind in general. In other words, it could be the human number. The Greek contains no article such as "a" or "the." Since it doesn't say the number of *the* man, John didn't have a specific person in mind, such as the Roman emperor Nero. The original text doesn't allow for that. But it could refer to an individual man or to human beings in general. Either possibility works grammatically in the original language.

What do we make of the number 666? One school of thought tries to identify the beast using the palindrome numbering system, in which letters are equated with numbers. Using this numbering system, people have sought to identify who is indicated by the letters in the 666 number. It turns out that many names line up, including Ronald Reagan, Martin Luther, Bill Gates, Prince Charles, Barney the purple dinosaur, the Holy Bible, and so on. These options can be quickly and randomly pulled from the Internet.[11] None of these individuals have any relation to the Bible record, however.

If the Bible really does interpret itself, why don't we stick with that? Remember, one of the tools in our interpretation toolbox is that John understood the vision he received. Whatever 666 turns out to be, John understood it at the time. So using only the Bible, here are some ideas of what John may have understood 666 to symbolize.

---

11. The Internet can be a great research tool when used correctly, and a terrible one when used incorrectly. Imagine the kind of smear campaigns that would have been offered up against Jesus and the prophets on the Internet if it had existed then. Malicious people smear godly people today.

Babylon's numbering system

Perhaps 666 could be considered the number of Babylon. Babylon rings all sorts of bells. Babylonians used a numbering system of sixes rather than tens. Perhaps 666 is supposed to make us recall Babylon. Well, that's one idea.

Six is incomplete

Here's another idea. The number six is short of seven, which in the Bible means completion or perfection. Seven is God's number in Revelation, so perhaps 666 represents not measuring up or falling short of God's plan.

Half of twelve

The number six is half of twelve. Twelve represents the people of God in Revelation. It's a combination of three, the number of the trinity, and four, the number of the earth (the four points of the compass). Three times four equals twelve, and three plus four equals seven. Both twelve and seven are significant numbers on God's side. So maybe the number six is a portrayal of the opposing side.

The sixth day of creation

Here's another possibility. Human beings were created on the sixth day of creation. So was the serpent. Serpents and dragons are slithering all over in Revelation, so perhaps the number 666 caused John to think in terms of the sixth day of creation as the human number. We do have allusions to creation elsewhere, so it could be a hint.

The counterfeit trinity

This number could represent the counterfeit trinity. Each of them—the dragon, the sea beast, and the land beast—may be connected to the number six, as man is, because animals were created on the sixth day, and the three of them together might make three sixes. Could the number 666 be a numerical representation of the counterfeit trinity seeking to take the place of God?

Solomon's paycheck

The number 666 as a complete unit occurs only one other place in the Bible. In 1 Kings 10:14 we read that Solomon's income each year was 666

97

talents of gold. So what? In Hebrew thinking, an allusion points to a larger story. The larger context of Solomon's income of 666 talents is the Queen of Sheba's visit at the height of his power. She notes Solomon's wisdom, power, and wealth and comes to him to get to know the true God. This amount of 666 talents comes just before Solomon's wives draw him away from the true God and he begins to build temples to false gods.

Revelation's pointing to 666 could be an allusion to the apostasy of Solomon, the son of David, who fell away and became an opponent of the true God. Could it be that this number points to the sea beast as one who is actually God's work and God's people gone bad? This beast is, after all, wearing a Christian face. It portrays itself to the world as the work of God in Jesus Christ, even though it's all a counterfeit.

Nebuchadnezzar's image

Here's one more possibility. Maybe this number is an allusion to Daniel 3. It's difficult to get away from the story of Daniel 3 when reading Revelation 13:12–18. In the story, everyone was forced to worship an image upon pain of death. The dimensions of the image in Daniel 3 are described in sixes: 60 cubits high, 6 cubits wide, and presumably 6 cubits deep. So possibly the number 666 is an allusion to that story as a parallel to how the end-time scenario will play out: the creation of an image, an order to worship it, and death to anyone who disobeys.

Summary

Wherever we come down on the interpretation of this number, remember that it made sense to John and to the believers in the seven churches. That realization alone rules out theories about credit cards or whatever else we might have invented since those days.

Don't get frustrated if symbols aren't becoming clear just yet. We're still working on the big story. Identifying all of the symbols up front can actually serve as a barrier to seeing the full story. We're much more likely to get the whole story using the pictures that are there and later filling in unclear details. Know the whole story first, and then try to interpret it.

So hang in there. This will get clearer and clearer as we go on.

Study Guide Outline

Chapter 10

1. Revelation 12:17 sets the stage for the final _____ of earth's history.

2. Before diving into the dragon's side of the battle, Revelation describes the new character: the beast from the _____.

3. The _____ of Greek grammar support this structure of Revelation 13.

4. The sea beast of Revelation 13 is a _____ of the beasts of Daniel 7.

5. The animals in Daniel's vision were all _____ powers.

6. The sea beast has a background of political power, but the fact that it also blasphemes God is a strong clue that this is also a _____ power.

7. The fatal wound and resurrection of the sea beast is a _____ of the death and resurrection of Jesus.

8. The dragon gives _____ to the sea beast and seems to be setting itself up to be a counterfeit of God the Father.

9. The clues concerning the identity of the beast are piling up:

    a. played a powerful _____ and political role for more than 1,000 years;

    b. entered a time of _____;

    c. has the potential of being _____ into power again;

    d. has a history of _____ of other Christians;

e. will have a rival _____ with a Christian message.

10. The land beast starts out good, but in the end it supports the dragon.

    a. It has no significant _____.

    b. It points the earth toward the sea beast by forcing people to _____ it.

    c. It brings _____ down from heaven.

    d. It creates an _____ and breathes life into it.

11. The primary issue in the final conflict will be _____.

12. The mark of the beast is a _____ to the seal of God (Revelation 7 and 14).

13. The mark of the beast and seal of God are signs of _____ to one or the other.

14. One of the best _____ explanations of 666 may lie in the story of Nebuchadnezzar's image in Daniel 3: the creation of an image, an order to worship it, and death to any who refuse.

Chapter 11

God's Side of the Battle

Revelation 14

Revelation 13 is a description of the final conflict from the dragon's side, while Revelation 14 describes the final conflict from the side of God and his people. A horrendous conspiracy is starting to take shape against God and his people, and chapter 14 details the response of his people to the actions of the counterfeit trinity.

Next we will look at who God's end-time people will be, what they will be like, and what their actions will be in the context of the final conflict.

Identity of God's end-time people

A number of different theories claim to define who makes up the people of God, or the remnant as they are often called, described in Revelation 12:17. The word *remnant* is used in the King James Version of the Bible. "And the dragon was wroth with the woman, and went to make war with the remnant of her seed, which keep the commandments of God, and have the testimony of Jesus Christ."

The dictionary definition of the original Greek word, *loipos,* is "the rest" or "the remaining ones." Who is it that makes up the rest or the remaining ones in Revelation? Is it the people of the seven churches who first read Revelation? They certainly must have believed they were a part of God's remnant people. After all, what Christian doesn't consider himself or herself to be part of God's remnant people? We all do. But is that the ultimate meaning of the text?

Some say that God's remnant people are a specific Christian denomination. Others think God's remnant people are all Christians of all ages. Still others say God's remnant people are an unknown end-time entity that doesn't exist yet.

So which of these theories, if any, is correct? Who are God's last-day people in Revelation 14, who will see through the deception of the counterfeit trinity?

Let's go to the text and see what clues are given outright. We can identify several marks that are provided for us. Remember we are still working
in the context of Revelation 12:17, which places us in the time of the final
conflict at the end of time. In that verse alone we already have two major
clues as to the identity of the remnant: they keep the commandments of
God and have the testimony of Jesus. Those are two of the most important identifying characteristics of God's last-day remnant people.

Mark 1: Keep all the commandments

Nearly everyone knows that the commandments were God's laws
given at Mt. Sinai to ancient Israel. With his own finger, God burned the
ten statutes onto two stone tablets and gave them to Moses. Make no mistake, though; the commandments were not new to Israel. Even a cursory
investigation of the Old Testament reveals that those laws had been in effect since the beginning of the world, though they were not written down
as far as we know. Since God was creating for himself a nation in Israel, he
codified ten moral laws and gave them to his people in writing.

Given that keeping the commandments is emphasized in Revelation,
would it be common sense to say that God's end-time people would keep
all of the commandments or just some of them? Most criminals in prison
are not guilty of murder, and since they have not murdered anyone, they
must keep some of the commandments—legally speaking, if not in the
spirit of the law.

Would it make sense that God's remnant church is known for keeping
some of the commandments? That's clearly ludicrous. It makes most sense
that one of the identifying marks of God's remnant people is a desire and
an effort to be faithful to all of the commandments. So that's mark number one: God's end-time remnant people keep all of the commandments.

Mark 2: Have the testimony of Jesus

We don't have to guess what the testimony of Jesus is. When John
attempted to worship the angel speaking to him, the angel wouldn't allow
it: "At this I fell at his feet to worship him. But he said to me, 'Do not do
it! I am a fellow servant with you and with your brothers who hold to *the
testimony of Jesus*. Worship God! For the testimony of Jesus is the spirit of
prophecy'" (Revelation 19:10).

John and his brothers had the testimony of Jesus, which is the spirit
of prophecy. The angel further expands this in Revelation 22:9, when John

tries again to worship the angel. It seems he didn't learn the first time. "But he said to me, 'Do not do it! I am a fellow servant with you and with *your brothers the prophets* and of all who keep the words of this book. Worship God!' "

John's brothers are the prophets down through the ages, and what John and his brothers the prophets had in common was the testimony of Jesus—the spirit or the gift of prophecy. So the first two marks of God's end-time remnant people are that they obey all of God's commandments and they have the gift of prophecy among them.

No more prophets?

Some people believe that the gift of prophecy is not alive and well today and that no more prophets will be sent before Jesus comes. But given the description of God's last-day people, what should we understand about that theory? The gift of prophecy will continue to bless us all the way to the end of time. We must accept the potential for the appearance of modern-day prophets, because one of the marks of God's last-day people is that the gift will be exhibited among them.

In light of Revelation 12:17, anyone looking to involve themselves in any Christian group ought to ask at least two foundational questions: (1) is this group keeping all of the commandments, and (2) do they at least acknowledge the potential for modern-day prophets?

Of course, we have to be careful with the gift of prophecy, as with any other gift of the Spirit. Some people take it to extremes. Also, where there are true prophets, there are always false prophets. As Jesus warned, "False Christs and false prophets will appear." Even while we accept the possibility of a modern-day prophet, we must be careful not to accept the prophetic claim lightly. Jesus warned us that we must discern between true and false prophets even today.

This why we have biblical tests for identifying true prophets. It behooves us to apply the tests to anyone claiming the gift, because if God sends a prophet we don't want to miss it, and if someone is a false prophet, we want to recognize that as well.

Some meet the criteria for the remnant

With just those two characteristics listed in Revelation 12:17, some Christians could feel good about their ideas concerning the identity of the remnant of Revelation. God has always had a called, chosen, remnant people, and the churches of John's day certainly met those first two criteria. They had John among them with the gift of prophecy, and they kept all the commandments, including the Sabbath commandment. That didn't change for some three hundred years after the deaths of Jesus and the twelve apostles.

However, this part of Revelation is concerned with the last days of earth's history. It's impossible that the churches of John's day could be the last-day remnant since they were not living in the time of the end. There must be a deeper meaning to the remnant in this part of Revelation.

Neither can Christians throughout history honestly claim to belong to this remnant group because not all Christians can claim to keep all the commandments or that they have the gift of prophecy among them. Our candidates for God's end-time remnant are dwindling.

Mark 3: Object of worldwide interest

Another characteristic of the remnant narrows the field even further. In Revelation 16:14 the dragon gathers the forces of the entire world against the remnant, which means that the remnant described here are the object of worldwide attention. How can a small group of people capture the attention of the world's leaders? It's not impossible, because terrorists have managed it already. Terrorists are a small group of people who have drawn attention so significantly that the countries of the world (generally) cooperate to fight them, spending billions of dollars. It's possible for a small minority to capture the notice of world powers.

From the text it's clear that this will be the situation of God's remnant people at the time of the end. They will hold the attention of the world's leaders (though not with violent terrorist attacks, of course).

Who can make this claim? What group of people is so well known worldwide that it (1) holds the attention of the world's leaders, (2) keeps all of the Ten Commandments, and (3) claims to have the gift of prophecy among them? No one.

So at this point, we're left with the option that in this part of Revelation, we are seeing an end-time group that doesn't yet exist in its final form. That said, the group that will become the end-time remnant exists even now, because God has had an unbroken line of his remnant people since the beginning of sin until today. The end-time remnant is still in the process of developing, and some of those developments won't take place until the very end.

Mark 4: Object of sanctions

Another characteristic of God's end-time remnant people shows up in Revelation 13:15–17. The dragon makes it impossible for this group to buy and sell. It places economic sanctions against them.

Mark 5: Focus of worldwide coalition

In Revelation 17:14 this end-time remnant is the focus of a worldwide coalition. The nations of the earth come together in cooperation against this group. We will see in Revelation 17 how the powers of the world will unite in the common purpose of destroying the remnant group.

Mark 6: Carry a significant message

In Revelation 14:7, the first angel's message, this group has a special message that goes to every nation, tribe, language, and people. That means their message is significant to the entire world.

No one currently carries a message that is significant to everyone. Christians know that the gospel message ought to be significant to everyone, but many people don't think of it as so. Consider, for example, the 10/40 Window area of the world, across Asia mostly, where two-thirds of the world's population lives. Christians make up only 1 percent of that population. The people in this region don't consider the gospel message to be significant.

Remnant is much bigger

The impression we get when we put all of this information together is that the remnant described in Revelation is something different than anything that now exists in its current form. Here is a definition of the remnant of Revelation proposed by Dr. Jon Paulien: "The remnant of Revelation would seem to be a worldwide, spiritual, last-day group drawn from every worldwide organization and government." [12]

God's end-time remnant church is a group of people made of every nation, every language, and every ethnic group, who come together on the basis of the special proclamation of the gospel during the very last days of earth's history. The group is worldwide and it is spiritual, meaning that the people are marked by their character and message rather than by their

12. Jon Paulien. "Exegesis of the English New Testament: Revelation," Class lecture, Andrews University, Berrien Springs, MI. 2006.

affiliation with any particular organization. There's nothing wrong with organization, of course; God's people have historically been organized and will continue to be until it's impossible to remain so. If the predictions of Revelation are true, organization won't always be possible. What organization can continue to operate without being allowed to buy or sell and with all its leaders on "Wanted" posters everywhere?

The seeds of the end-time remnant exist

Since God has always had a chosen people, it must be from this group that the end-time remnant will come. The seeds of that group already exist today. Those who have seized hold of the message of Revelation and have put the gospel/prophecy/sanctuary package together (as we discussed in chapter 9) are the ones prophesied to bring on this last-day remnant that we see described here. And what they are doing is calling people to recognize the time in which we live, to get into the Scriptures and especially Revelation, to enter into a saving relationship with Jesus Christ, and to obey all of the commandments.

We must admit that not many people are pointing in this direction. Not many people attempt to keep all ten of the Commandments. Not many people recognize the possibility that the gift of prophecy could be among them. Yet these are clearly vital questions that every one of us should ask if we wish to be a part of the movement that brings on God's last-day remnant people.

And if we can't find anyone like that around us, then why not become the beginning of that movement ourselves? Why not move in that direction? Remember, prophecy is not so much intended to fill in every detail about the future as it is meant to give us enough information that we will re-prioritize our lives today. This information should make a difference in our lives beginning immediately. Let's get together and bring on this final movement.

Study Guide Outline

Chapter 11

1. Revelation is a description of the final _____ from the side of God and his people.

2. The marks of God's end-time remnant people include:

    a. Mark 1: They keep all the _____.

    b. Mark 2: The have the _____ of Jesus, which is the gift of prophecy.

    c. Mark 3: They are the object of worldwide _____.

    d. Mark 4: They are the object of economic _____.

    e. Mark 5: They are the focus of a worldwide _____ of opposition.

    f. Mark 6: They carry a message _____ to the entire world.

3. "The remnant of Revelation would seem to be a worldwide, spiritual, _____ group drawn from every worldwide organization and government" (Jon Paulien).

4. The remnant of Revelation seems to be marked by its character and its message rather than by affiliation with any particular _____.

5. It seems that the last-day remnant of Revelation does not yet _____ in its final form.

Chapter 12

The Character of the Remnant

Revelation 14, Part 2

Everyone knows that in Christian organizations, not every member is a true disciple of Jesus Christ. As time winds down, the situation will become even murkier, and even the nature of the organization will not be a reliable indicator of truth. After all, the beast arising from the sea appears to be a Christian organization, yet it will lead people astray. Anyone wishing to belong to God's last-day remnant people must pay close attention to the message and the character of anyone claiming to be part of that group.

Let's look specifically at what Revelation says about the character of the remnant. "Then I looked, and there before me was the Lamb, standing on Mount Zion, and with him 144,000 who had his name and his Father's name written on their foreheads" (Revelation 14:1).

Who are the 144,000 people in this verse? Are they the same group as the remnant? A subcategory of the remnant? Or an entirely separate group? Once again, allusion comes to the rescue. The answer is pretty clear from Joel 2:32. You can tell this is a commonly accepted allusion because Bible cross-references list it. "Everyone who calls on the name of the LORD will be saved; for on Mount Zion and in Jerusalem there will be deliverance, as the LORD has said, among the survivors whom the LORD calls."

The prophet Joel describes a remnant from Jerusalem, called "survivors" in this translation. They call on the name of the Lord and stand on Mt. Zion. There isn't any question that John in Revelation is recalling this scene. He sees the remnant standing on Mt. Zion and in relation to the Father's name that is written on their foreheads. This is also called the seal of God in Revelation. But Revelation makes one change from Joel. Instead of calling them "remnant" or "those that remain," it calls them the 144,000.

Considering that the last place we saw God's end-time people was in Revelation 12:17, this passage seems to tell us this is the same group. And if you study Revelation 7 carefully you will also find that the great multitude that could not be numbered is also this same group. That's at least three different ways of describing the end-time remnant in Revelation. This is typical for Revelation; it often uses different symbols for the same object.

If in fact the 144,000 and the great multitude that could not be numbered are the same group, what does that tell us about the 144,000? Is it a literal number or a symbolic number? It must be symbolic.

Reflect Jesus' character

Names are often significant in Scripture, and each of these different names for the remnant provides different clues about the character of the people. Also, they have the name of the Lamb and His Father's name written on their foreheads. In Old Testament times, marking on the forehead was recognition of that person's character. So in John's thinking, having the names of the Lamb and the Father on the forehead means reflecting the character of God.

What does that look like? Our character is revealed in our actions. Take Jesus, for example. His actions revealed his true character. His actions backed up His words and gave them credibility. The truth is, if you take Jesus at his words alone, he may seem to come off looking the part of a sissy. "Be nice to people. If someone slaps you, don't fight back. Don't worry about providing for your family because the birds and flowers don't work. Love your enemies," and so on. We wonder why men are often less enthusiastic about the Christian religion than women in our Western culture. Could this be one of the reasons? *If this is what Jesus thinks a man should be, then give me tackle football, hunting, and wrestling.*

Of course, this perception comes from a devil-inspired misunderstanding of the character of Jesus. Jesus was anything but a spineless wimp.

Jesus was strong. He was strong enough to go 40 days without food. How many men can do that? He was strong enough to spend entire nights in prayer. He was strong enough to not hit back, which takes more strength than fighting back. Jesus was strong enough to resist everything the devil threw at him in Gethsemane. He was strong enough to take brutal lashings and still give a good effort to carrying his own cross.

Jesus had authority. A few words from him, and the temple emptied. A few words from him, and his enemies were silenced.

Jesus was fearless. He was fearless enough to stand firm as crazed madmen rushed at him. Tough guys Peter, James, and John fled. Jesus was fearless enough to sleep through a life-threatening storm. He was fearless enough to say, "Not my will, Father, but yours be done." That took serious guts.

Jesus was courageous. He was courageous enough to stand alone. He was courageous enough to go against the popular way. He was courageous enough to not fight those who hurt him. He was courageous enough to stand firm before the whip, courageous enough to take the pain in silence as nails were pounded through his hands and feet, courageous enough to forgive, and to die for people who hated him.

That's but a small sample of the kind of character Jesus modeled as a true man. It is the kind of character his people will strive to gain: fearlessly upholding truth, courageously standing in the minority if necessary, authoritatively preaching what God is really about, strongly resisting the urge to fight using the devil's tactics.

Do not believe the lie that Satan has sold to this planet about what it means to be true men and women! Jesus, the one who designed and created us, showed us what that is really all about.

The remnant is loyal to God

The next characteristic of God's remnant people is found in Revelation 14:4. "These are those who did not defile themselves with women, for they kept themselves pure." This is sexual imagery, which is common Old Testament language concerning loyalty to God. When Old Testament Israel started to serve other gods, prophets such as Isaiah, Jeremiah, and Ezekiel showed up using the language of adultery, prostitution, and sexual unfaithfulness to describe what Israel was doing to God in their spiritual unfaithfulness.

For those acquainted with Old Testament imagery and language, this idea in Revelation 14:4 of not being defiled by women is clearly not a commentary on the sexuality of God's people but an image of loyalty to God.

They are in continuous relationship

Revelation 14:4 goes on to say, "They follow the Lamb wherever he goes." In other words, they are in continuous relationship with Jesus. This means much more than a point-to-the-date conversion when they were "saved" and that was the end of it. It's not just a one-hour, once-a-week-at-11:00-a.m. relationship. It is a continual, constant, unceasing relationship with Jesus, which marks the character of God's remnant people.

The remnant is serious about the relationship. They intentionally work on it just as people with strong marriages work on their relationship. God's people spend lots of time in His word. They spend time in prayer. They spend time alone with God. They discipline themselves physically and mentally because they understand the effect this has on them spiritually. They are disciples of Jesus, growing daily in him.

They are authentic

"No lie was found in their mouths," Revelation 4:5 says. Does that mean if you have ever told a fib, you're sunk? No. The letter to Laodicea in Revelation 3 shows something clearly: the church of Laodicea is lying. They say they are rich and need nothing, but the truth is that they are pitiful, poor, blind, and naked.

Now, odd as it may seem, Bible scholars recognize that the 144,000 are part of Laodicea. How in the world do we put those two together? What's the connection between the remnant with the character of Jesus and the Laodiceans who are lukewarm and pitiful? The connection is possible because even though they are part of Laodicea, the remnant is authentic about their true condition.

We take a tremendous step toward becoming part of God's remnant people when we're willing to admit the truth about ourselves—that we are wretched, poor, pitiful, blind, and naked. When we admit that we are messed-up people who need Jesus Christ for everything, then we are telling the truth. There is no lie in us. We are no longer claiming to have some sort of righteousness before God.

The double message of the cross

The message of the gospel has two edges. The first message is that we are wretched, pitiful, poor, blind, and naked. In short, we are lost. The second message is that in spite of our lost condition, we are acceptable to God in Jesus Christ. At Jesus' death on the cross, God condemned the sinful condition of the human race, but then at the resurrection of Jesus, God accepted the human race in Jesus. The beauty of the gospel is that the more hurt we are by our own condition, the more clearly we understand that in Christ we are acceptable to God.

So God's last day people will be authentic about their condition and admit their serious brokenness. They will strive to walk more closely with Jesus in the knowledge that in him we can be saved.

Revelation 14:5 also says the remnant people are blameless. It doesn't say sinless. It doesn't mean that they don't struggle with sin and temptation but that they are completely loyal to God. When we are loyal, we are blameless even when we make mistakes. Making mistakes is different than disobedience.

Our children are not perfect, but as long as they are doing their best, as long as they are consistently maturing into well-rounded adults, then they are blameless. They may make mistakes, but they are not rebelling. Blamelessness means consistent spiritual growth and maturity. We are blameless as long as we are consistently progressing in that direction.

The good news is that you can be blameless right now by making the decision to be loyal to Jesus no matter what. Surrender your life to Jesus, even if it's for the thousandth time. Give Jesus permission to come into your life and transform you. You don't have to understand completely how he does it; simply give him permission to do what you may not understand. If you sincerely do that right now, you will be blameless. The gospel truly is good news.

The message of the remnant

Now let's look at the message that, according to Revelation 14, God's people will be delivering during the time of the end. "Then I saw another angel flying in midair, and he had the eternal gospel to proclaim to those who live on the earth—to every nation, tribe, language and people" (Revelation 14:6).

This is one part of the three angels' messages, which we have already seen represent evangelism (the mystery of God) going to the world in the last days. As this final message is going out, it is a message grounded in the gospel. No matter what the remnant talk about, be it prophecy or the sanctuary or anything else, it is always grounded in the gospel—the story of how Jesus came to earth, lived his life as an example for us, overcame sin, suffered for our sins and died on a cross, and rose again, all in order to overcome evil and save us. All paths lead to the good news as it is in Jesus.

This proclamation of the gospel will go to the entire world, as Revelation 10:11 states. But we're talking about the end of time, so even though the gospel has been proclaimed since the time of Jesus, the message of the remnant will have particular significance for the time of the end.

The heart of that final message is found in Revelation 14:7. "He said in a loud voice, 'Fear God and give him glory, because the hour of his judgment has come. Worship him who made the heavens, the earth, the sea and the springs of water.'"

The gospel message that the remnant is carrying to the world is three commands: fear God, give him glory, and worship him. Why? Because the hour of his judgment has come.

Judgment has come

Remember in Revelation 13 how the tenses were important because they told us the time frame in which we were looking. Here is the same situation. The hour of God's judgment *has* come. So far in Revelation's prophecy, the Second Coming has not yet occurred, but during the final proclamation of the gospel, judgment has already come. Judgment begins before the end.

We usually think of judgment as happening at the Second Coming, and that is partly true. But there is much more to judgment than what happens at the time of the Second Coming, just as there is much more to judgment in county court than the judge simply dropping his gavel and pronouncing a sentence.

The part of judgment referred to in verse 7 is not the sentencing phase of judgment. That phase does come at the second coming of Christ. The earlier phase is an investigative judgment, if you will. This is what those who studied the Old Testament sanctuary discovered, after they were so bitterly disappointed when Jesus didn't return. They discovered that the sanctuary being cleansed alluded to the Day of Atonement, a day of judgment for Israel.

Think of it this way. For a prisoner, one part of judgment has finished when he is released. He went to prison for his crime, and then he is freed on parole and probation. But he's not freed entirely. He has paid the penalty for his crime, but in a way judgment has arrived all over again for him. He will be watched and evaluated during this time to see if eventually he will be allowed to go entirely free. The judge is asking the question, *Has there been a change of heart in this criminal?*

While he's on parole, the verdict is still in the future, but judgment time has arrived. That is what the time of the end is all about. It is preparation for sentencing. This is what we're seeing in this text and throughout Scripture. Judgment has arrived for us. We are pardoned sinners thanks to

Jesus' death on the cross for us. However, we are still facing judgment in which the question is asked, *Has there been a change of heart? Are our actions proving that there's been a change of heart?*

If what we're seeing here in Revelation is right, this part of the gospel message will gain prominence the closer we get to the end of time. After all, this is what makes the end-time message so urgent. Judgment has already begun! Sit up! Take note! The court in heaven has been seated. Probation is open. Investigation is underway. Soon Jesus will return for the sentencing phase of judgment.

The Bible reveals at least three different types of judgment.

First there was judgment at the cross (see John 12:31–32; Romans 8:3; Acts 13:32–33). In the person of Jesus Christ, the entire human race was judged negatively at the cross and then judged positively at the resurrection. In Jesus Christ, God rejected us at the cross, and then in Jesus Christ he accepted us at the resurrection. That was a judgment situation. So judgment upon the human race happened at the cross.

The next time of judgment happens every time the cross is preached (see John 3:18–21; John 5:22–25; Matthew 18:18). It is a time of judgment for those who hear that message because they must make a choice. They can't be neutral or ignore that sermon. They must either agree and accept what Jesus did on the cross for them, or they must reject it. Every time we talk about the cross of Christ, people must either be drawn closer to Jesus or be driven further away.

Finally, there is judgment at the end, in relation to the Second Coming (see John 12:48; Acts 17:31; John 5:28–29).

Ultimately, we pass judgment on ourselves by accepting or rejecting Jesus Christ during the course of our lives every time we consider the cross of Christ. The final judgment merely ratifies our own decision. If we reject him, the judge essentially says, "I don't like your decision, but it's yours to make." The gavel falls, and our fate is sealed.

In Revelation 6:10 the saints call out, "How long will you not be judging?" Near the end, in Revelation 19:2, which is still before the Second Coming, judgment is finished. All that's left is the implementation of the sentencing.

The message of judgment is a call to be accountable to God right now. Judgment time is here, and it's not over yet; it is currently in process.

This gives 2 Corinthians 6:2 some teeth. Paul says, "Now is the day of God's favor. Now is the day of salvation." Just like parole for a prisoner, this investigative phase of judgment is a call to special accountability before God.

Accountability

But we do not like accountability. Unfortunately, little good is accomplished without it. Accountability provides structure for the ordinary duties of life. Jesus said that if you give a cup of cold water to a child it will be remembered in the day of judgment (Matthew 10:42). Every little action matters to God, whether it's chipping ice off the sidewalk, caring for a child in the middle of the night, or cooking a meal for your family. All will be remembered at the judgment. Nothing you do is unimportant. Everything matters.

Let's be clear, though, that accountability and good actions do not earn salvation for us. Salvation is a free gift of grace. Accountability is the *evidence* that we have had a change of heart. It's our response to the incredible gift of salvation.

If we accept God's gift of grace, this kind of judgment is great news, as it is for the prisoner on parole who has had a change of heart. For the faithful, judgment is something to look forward to, not to dread.

The analogy of the prisoner on parole does leave out one crucial element. For those of us who have had a change of heart and accepted Jesus' sacrifice in our place, in this investigative phase of judgment the judge isn't looking at our performance at all. He's looking at Jesus Christ's performance. All we have to do is accept him in our place. If we will allow Jesus to be our righteousness by accepting the gift he gave us on the cross, we have nothing to fear of judgment. Indeed, we look forward to judgment, the day God sets the injustices right.

Judgment sets things right

Judgment is the time of fixing everything that was broken during the reign of sin on planet earth. We are powerless to set things right. We can't change the genocide in Rwanda. We can't undo child abuse. We can't fix what has been broken. But in the judgment, God will set everything right. The injustices of life—torture, rape, murder, everything—God will make right. If you have been the victim of wrongs, God will make it right.

We may not see now how God can do that. It may seem that nothing short of a miracle that could set right what happened to us. But our God is a God of miracles. Nothing is impossible for him. He has never failed, and if he says he will make things right, he will make things right.

Some people are afraid of judgment, but next to the gospel itself, judgment is the best news you can bring to anyone. God is going to set right every wrong that has happened on planet earth.

The only people who need fear judgment are those who have chosen not to accept the covering righteousness of Jesus Christ, those who are unfaithful to what they know to be right, those who are not loyal to the Lamb of Revelation.

You don't have to get revenge in this life. God says, "Vengeance is mine." And he will do it right. That's judgment, and that's good news for God's people!

Judgment is the reason God's last-day people are preaching the messages of the three angels in Revelation 14. However, in verse 7, judgment isn't the primary message. It's mostly a time locator, telling us where we are in this process of judgment. The primary message in the verse is to fear God, give Him glory, and worship Him. Anyone who does that has no fear of the judgment.

Study Guide Outline

Chapter 12

1. The remnant, the _____, and the great multitude that cannot be numbered are different names for the same group of people.

2. The remnant of Revelation will reflect the _____ of Jesus, including strength, authority, courage, and fearlessness.

3. "Kept themselves pure" refers to _____ to God.

4. "Following the Lamb wherever he goes" refers to a continuous _____ with Jesus.

5. "No lie was found in their mouths" indicates the fact that God's people will be _____ about their true condition.

6. The double message of the cross is that because of our condition, we are _____, but regardless of that condition, we are acceptable to God in Jesus.

7. "They are blameless" refers to the fact that God's people are _____ like Jesus.

8. We can be blameless right now simply by giving Jesus permission to begin his work of _____ our lives.

9. The three angels' messages represent the _____ going to the world: evangelism.

10. The final message of God's last-day people will be grounded in the _____.

11. The three major commands of Revelation 14:7 are: _____ God, _____ him glory, and _____ him.

12. We should pay attention to these commands because judgment has already begun during the time of the final _____ of the gospel.

13. The three times of judgment are:

    a.   At the _____

    b.   Each time the cross is _____

    c.   _____ at the end.

14. This pre-Advent judgment is a call to be _____ to God in even the little things of life.

15. Judgment will set _____ right again.

Chapter 13

The Seal of God

Revelation 14, Part 3

It's interesting how often people ask about the mark of the beast but never ask about its opposite, the seal of God. If we can track down what the seal of God is, then we're going to know clearly what the counterfeit is.

What we will see now has a way of turning a lot of preconceived ideas on their head, but we can't get around this part of the story because it's the pivotal point of Revelation. The entire deception of the unholy trinity hinges on the choice people will one day be forced to make, between the seal of God and mark of the beast.

We are still working in the context of the final conflict, where the dragon and his two allies are attacking God's people through a deception that, if possible, Jesus said, could deceive even the elect. We should expect an exceptionally convincing counterfeit.

It's such a strong deception because it appears to be provable at least on some level by the Bible itself. It has a Christian face. It includes a counterfeit trinity with impersonations of God the Father, Jesus, and the Holy Spirit. It works miracles that only God is supposed to be able to do. God's people will tremble at how convincing this deception will be. The crux of the deception will concern worship, as we will see, and its purpose will be to convince the earth to worship a false god.

So this is the context: a great end-time deception.

In the last chapter we saw that during these times, God's remnant people will be delivering a specific kind of gospel message geared for the end of time. "He said in a loud voice, 'Fear God and give him glory, because the hour of his judgment has come. Worship him who made the heavens, the earth, the sea and the springs of water' " (Revelation 14:7). The point of the text, as we just saw, is the message in the context of judgment.

Fear God by taking him seriously

The message of the end time remnant calls people to fear God. What does that mean? The word *fear* loses something in translation and over time. To fear God is not to be afraid of God. Rather it is to respect, admire, to be focused on God, to concentrate on God. To fear God is to take God seriously. God is calling to the world through his remnant messengers to take him seriously, to be accountable to him, to make him the object of our attention.

Fear God by being in relationship with him

The Old Testament contains several parallel texts for this idea of fearing God. One is Proverbs 9:10: "The fear of the LORD is the beginning of wisdom, and knowledge of the Holy One is understanding."

In Hebrew poetry the author states the first line then repeats the same statement using different words; therefore, the proverb is equating the fear of the Lord with knowledge of the Lord.

When the Bible speaks of knowing, it's not referring to casual acquaintance. For instance, the King James Bible says that Adam *knew* Eve, and out of that knowing, a son was born. So knowing his wife was pretty intimate. Knowing God isn't just knowing about God on an intellectual level; it is knowing him intimately. To fear God is be in deep relationship with him.

Fear God by obeying him

Psalm 111:10 says that to fear God is to keep his commandments. First John 2:3 tells us that we know him if we keep his commandments. This is the very thing the remnant people are doing in Revelation 12:17: keeping his commandments. God calls out through his messengers for the people of the world to fear him, to be in relationship with him, and in that relationship to obey him by being loyal to all of his commandments.

Fear God by avoiding evil

We find another concept concerning the fear of God in Proverbs 3:7 and 16:6. To fear God includes avoiding evil. Does that mean not murdering, not stealing, not committing adultery? It does when we understand the Ten Commandments in the broad way that Jesus explained them on the Sermon on the Mount. He showed us that killing includes more than literal killing and that adultery is more than just cheating on your spouse.

The rest of the Bible expands on what it means to avoid evil. For instance, Paul, in Philippians 4:8 says, "Finally, brothers, whatever is true, whatever is noble, whatever is right, whatever is pure, whatever is lovely, whatever is admirable—if anything is excellent or praiseworthy—think about such things."

A mother won't let her child do something, and the kid whines, "Why? What's wrong with it?"

She asks in reply, "What is right with it?"

He says, "Nothing."

She says, "Then that is what is wrong with it."

The heart that wants to avoid hell but isn't very interested in God will see Paul's counsel in a negative light. That heart thinks, *Oh boy, just look at everything I want to do that I can't do. I can't do this and that and that. What's wrong with those things? Where's the fun in such a life? The great cost of following Jesus is just too high.*

Whereas the heart that is loyal to Jesus sees such counsel in a positive light. *Wow, just look at everything good that is open to me! Just like Augustine said, I can love God and do whatever I please. Because I love God, I want to do what is true and right. Where is the fun in slavery to sin compared to this? The small cost of following Jesus is well worth it. What a bargain!*

All of these concepts—fearing God in relationship, intimacy, obedience, and avoiding evil—connect to the message God's remnant people are carrying to the world that everyone should take God seriously because the hour of his judgment is already here, and sometime very soon we are going to be held accountable for our lives.

Every day we can take God more seriously than we did the day before. We can learn what it means to become more intimate with God; consciously avoid evil; learn what he expects of us; and become obedient to him. We cannot be loyal *and* disobedient. "If you love me," said Jesus, "you will obey me."

Judgment is here! We're on parole, in a manner of speaking. God is looking at hearts right now. Has there been a change in your heart? He's not looking at your outward appearance the way everyone else is. He sees right through you. He's looking for a loyal heart. He is looking for those who love the truth.

Give him glory

The next part of the message God's people carry to the world is the command to give glory to God. What does it mean to give glory to God? Does it mean only praising him by waving our hands to music at church? Actually, this is a call to something much greater.

By nature we glory in ourselves: our possessions, our performance, and the important people we know. By nature we are self-focused. When we feel a need to boost our sense of self-worth, we do it by going shopping or seeking a promotion or glorying in who we know, or invading a small country if we have that kind of power.

The call to the final generation is a call to exalt the gospel (Romans 4:2–5), not to focus on ourselves. God's final messengers will make it clear that we are who we are because God has done exceptional things in us, not because we are exceptional people. We glorify God when we show who is doing the work in us.

The wonderful thing about legalism (which means trying to earn your salvation by your good deeds) is that the credit and the glory go to the one who does the work—you! But giving glory to God means recognizing and giving credit to God for the work he has done in us.

Another way we give glory to God is in our own healthy, vibrant life. "Do you not know that your body is a temple of the Holy Spirit, who is in you, whom you have received from God? You are not your own; you were bought at a price. Therefore honor God with your body" (1 Corinthians 6:19–20). We glorify or disgrace God in our body and in the way we behave, in the way we eat, the way we exercise. When we make our bodies into a place where the Holy Spirit can live vibrantly, we bring glory to God our creator. For this reason alone, every church and every person should emphasize physical health as a part of gospel outreach.

Another way to give God glory is by being grateful and positive. Some people have counted more than 3,000 passages in the Bible that tell us to be thankful and give praise to God. A big reason we don't spend our days in awe and gratitude to God is simply because we are blind to his blessings. We're grateful the day we get a new car, but the fact that the car didn't break down today is a blessing for which we should be equally grateful. If you are ever feeling down, stop and write ten things for which you're grateful and see if it doesn't improve your spirits.

Ultimately, giving God glory is a call to focus outside of ourselves. Life is about so much more than "me." Life is about God. Giving glory to God is part of the message of God's last-day messengers.

Worship him

The third part of the message that God's remnant people carry to the world is a message of worship. At earth's final crisis, a counterfeit trinity will be working on a deception, and that trinity is attacking the remnant. Notice the prominence of worship in Revelation 13:4, 8, 12, 15. Five times in Revelation 13 the word *worship* occurs. Then in Revelation 14:9, 11 it occurs twice more.

We have already seen how the number 7 is extremely important in the Bible and in Revelation in particular. So, could the fact that the word *worship* appears seven times in this part of Revelation be coincidence? Yes, it could be, but at this point we might be beyond coincidence. At least one scholar believes that in Revelation, words appear in threes, fours, and sevens often enough that coincidence seems unlikely.

Another interesting fact: in these seven instances where worship is mentioned in the context of the final conflict, only one instance refers to God. The others refer to worshiping the beast. So, if it really is significant that worship is mentioned seven times, that would mean John counted them and realized that he had used it six times in relation to the beast and once in relation to God. That suggests to us that the one time it is mentioned in relation to God, it would be a crucial verse.

You'll remember how Revelation is structured in a chiasm, and the center of the book is the fulcrum, the tipping point, so to speak. The center of Revelation is chapters 12, 13, and 14 with a few verses on either end.

Center of the center

It appears that there is also a center of these three center chapters—a center of the center, if you will. The center of the center of Revelation, some scholars note, is the three angels' messages, which makes the passage that we're studying now the most crucial element of Revelation. We have all sorts of narrative about the dragon and the beast, but it is in the three angel's messages that God details the specific message relevant to the final crisis. This is the tipping point that you simply cannot ignore in Revelation.

Center of the center of the center

But wait! It may go deeper still. Some scholars believe they have identified a center of the center of the center in Revelation. If that's true then that center would be the single most important passage in the entire book of Revelation. That is what we likely have in Revelation 14:7. It says, "Fear

God and give him glory, for the hour of his judgment has come. Worship him who made heaven, earth, sea and fountains of water."

We have already established that worship is the primary focus of the last great deception, that Satan is counterfeiting the work of God point by point, and that his goal is that the people of earth will worship him in his way rather than worshiping the true God in his way. Judging by the structure of Revelation this is the central, most significant point in Revelation. It's the top of the chiasm. It's the center of the center of the center. Nothing could be more central to the message of Revelation than this particular verse. And it says of God, "Worship him."

It's time for our interpretation toolbox again. This time we're going to use every tool in it, because we want to be absolutely sure about what we encounter.

First we look for allusions. We begin by tracking down verbal parallels, and we have one in the words "made, heaven, earth, sea," and a reference to God. There is probably no place in Revelation that has verbal parallels with more than six or seven words in common with another passage of Scripture. Here we have four important words, which may not seem like much, but allusion works with even one parallel word if it's a unique word. We will discover that these four words in this order make one of the strongest verbal parallels in Revelation.

However, the presence of a verbal parallel doesn't necessarily mean the author intended to make an allusion. He could have just been using the same words accidently. We must be careful not to see something that isn't there. So, even though we see verbal parallels between this verse and another, it doesn't necessarily indicate an allusion.

We should take our analysis further. After verbal parallels, the next tool we will pull out is a check for thematic parallels, and we'll also check for structural parallels. The bottom line is that after putting this allusion through the most rigorous paces, we are going to be confident that, of all the allusions in Revelation, this one is the strongest, hands down. There will be no denying this allusion.

Let's go point by point through the verbal, thematic, and structural parallels and test them, because we want to be very sure we are on solid footing here.

Verbal parallel
"Worship Him who made the heavens, the earth, the sea, and the foun-

tains of water." We should recognize those words. If we don't, we need to memorize the Ten Commandments. They are the words of Exodus 20:11, the fourth commandment, "for in six days the Lord made the heavens, the earth, the sea, and all that is in them." This is parallel to Revelation 14:7.[13]

Thematic parallels

Does the theme of Revelation 14:7 have a common theme with this passage in Exodus 20? Yes, it does. Each of the first four commandments has a motivation built into it—a reason "why" you should keep this commandment. The fifth commandment has an obvious motivation. It says, "Honor your father and your mother." That's the command. But then it gives us a good reason for obeying. "So that your days may be long in the land that the Lord your God gives you." The motivation for honoring your parents is long life.

Each of the first four commandments also has a built-in motivation. The first commandment says, "I am the LORD your God, who brought you out of Egypt, out of the land of slavery. You shall have no other gods before me." The command: don't have other gods. Why? "Because I saved you, I brought you out of the land of Egypt. I am your salvation." There's a *salvation* theme in the first commandment.

The second commandment says, "Do not bow down to idols." Why? "Because I am a jealous God who visits the iniquity of the fathers on the children." In other words, "I am a God of judgment." Don't bow down to idols or you will be punished. There is a *judgment* theme in the second commandment.

The third commandment says, "Don't take God's name in vain." If you do, God will not hold you guiltless, which also sounds like a *judgment* theme.

The fourth commandment says, "Keep the Sabbath holy." Why? "Because I am the Creator. I made the heavens, the earth, the sea, and all that is in them. I'm the owner of everything. Obey me because I made you and you belong to me." This is no different than a reason we give to our kids in demanding their obedience. "Why, Dad?" "Because I am your father and

---

13. The connection between these two verses is noted by the United Bible Societies' critical Greek text, which is created by a multi-denominational panel as well as at least one secular scholar not associated with any denomination. So this verbal parallel is universally recognized.

you are my child. I made you. You belong to me." There is a *creation* theme in the fourth commandment.

Now look again at Revelation 14:6, 7: "I saw another angel flying in mid-heaven having the everlasting gospel." The gospel is about how God has saved us through Jesus Christ on the cross—a salvation theme, the same theme as the first commandment.

"And he said with a loud voice, 'Fear God and give him glory for the hour of his judgment has come.' " Just like the second and third commandments: a theme of judgment.

"Worship him who made the heavens, the earth, the sea and the springs of water." This is commandment number four, with a creation theme.

Thematically, Revelation 14:7 has the first four commandments in view, and even in the same order. The words are in the same order, and the ideas are in the same order. The verbal and thematic parallels are highly impressive. But something that is already strong becomes even stronger.

Structural parallels

After we look for verbal and thematic parallels, we look for structural parallels. Does this make sense in the overall structure? Does Revelation direct our attention to this idea in other places? Why would it to allude to commandments here?

Both Revelation 12:17 and 14:12 refer directly to the Commandments. So Revelation is clearly interested in the Commandments in this section specifically, and also elsewhere in the book. The Commandments are a consistent theme in Revelation. So structurally it makes perfect sense.

We've used all the tools, and yet there's one more fascinating confirmation of what we're seeing from the negative side.

The beast's counterfeit

In Revelation 13, the beast seems to be trying to counterfeit each of the first four commandments.

1. In Revelation 13 there are many calls to worship the beast. The first commandment is a call to worship only God. The beast is breaking the first commandment and calling on others to do the same.
2. Then the beast calls on people around the world to worship the image of the beast. Here is the second commandment, which specifically forbids creating images and bowing to them and worshiping them.
3. Then the beast is full of blasphemy. He blasphemes against God and

heaven and those who live in it. Blasphemy is a major characteristic of the beast, which reminds us of the third commandment, to not take God's name in vain.

4. And finally the beast creates a mark and places that mark on everyone.

Seal of the covenant

If you go back to ancient covenants, particularly Hittite covenants of the same era and region as the Ten Commandments, in the center of every covenant was a statement of who the ruler was, what his territory was, and what the relationship between him and his subjects was. So at the heart of every ancient covenant there was a seal, a central message, regarding the maker of the covenant.

This was standard operating procedure for the time that the Ten Commandments were written. This custom clearly appears in the fourth commandment. The Sabbath command is the seal of the covenant, and the beast counterfeits that with a mark of his own—a counterfeit fourth commandment, which commands people to worship on a different day. Remember, the dragon has been setting up this final deception for thousands of years. He is working everything toward an end.

We have already seen that the little-horn power in Daniel's vision is the same as the sea beast. Suddenly, the fact that this entity seeks to change times and laws becomes startlingly clear.

So at this decisive "center in a center in a center" point in the book of Revelation, we find a strong allusion to the fourth commandment. The response to God's call to worship Him as the true God is to do so in light of the Ten Commandments and the fourth commandment in particular.

So here we are in the context of the final battle of earth's history, and God's end-time messengers bring this special message connected to the fourth commandment. In response to the many calls to worship the beast comes the single call to worship God who gave the Ten Commandments, the ones He burned into stone with His own finger.

Does it make sense?

Now let's ask why. Does it make any sense for God to make an issue in the final conflict over which day we worship? After all, sincere Christians since the fourth century have been keeping Sunday. What sense would it make for God to make an issue of this at the very end?

When you think about it, we keep most of the commandments

whether or not we believe in God simply because it is in our best interest to do so. If I don't want to be murdered, I had better not go around murdering other people. If I don't want you stealing my stuff, I probably better not steal yours. If I don't want you chasing my wife, I probably shouldn't chase yours. Keeping most of the commandments is in our best interest.

The only seemingly arbitrary commandment is the day of worship. Perhaps the fourth commandment makes an ideal test of loyalty because there is no self-interest involved. There is no human reason for God to have picked Saturday to make holy more than Sunday or Tuesday. Neither does the fourth commandment make sense astronomically. Days, months, and years are governed by astronomy, but not weeks. The only reason for a week of seven days is that God made it so. Something as seemingly arbitrary as the Sabbath gives me no reason to obey except that God said to. It's a matter of loyalty to him.

Old covenant Sabbath?

But wait a minute. Didn't God do away with the Jewish Sabbath at the cross and give us Sunday in the new covenant? Well, there are a couple of major problems with that idea. First, there were no Jews when God created the Sabbath. There was only Adam and Eve. So right away we see that the Sabbath isn't only Jewish. The Sabbath is a marker of Creation, God's seal of his work. When he gave the Ten Commandments at Mt. Sinai, he prefaced the fourth with "Remember." They already knew about Sabbath and had known since Creation.

It's true that the Jewish ceremonial laws ended at the cross, but those were the laws that were fulfilled by the Messiah. All the laws that pointed to the Messiah would understandably be finished when he came. But the Sabbath didn't prefigure the Messiah; it recalled Creation.

The Christian church switched the day of worship in the fourth century after Christ. And the Roman Catholic Church still openly claims the authority to change such times and laws. Protestants are, quite frankly, acknowledging that Catholic authority by following along.

Disciples kept Sabbath

Wouldn't we expect that Jesus' disciples would have given up the Sabbath, if that was what Jesus had intended? We sometimes point to Paul preaching on Sunday, but he preached on any and every day of the week that afforded an opportunity. That doesn't change the Sabbath.

The Lord's Day

We also point to John being in the Spirit on the Lord's Day, but nowhere in the Bible is the Lord's Day equated with Sunday. It's not explicitly connected with any day. The closest connection to the Lord's Day comes when Jesus said that he was Lord of the Sabbath. So Sunday being the Lord's Day may be a nice tradition, but it has no biblical grounds.

The day changed

We've also heard that our calendar got messed up and the days got switched around, but again, that's not possible. Pope Gregory XIII adjusted the calendar in 1582. We had been operating by the calendar set up by Julius Caesar, which was discovered to be 11 minutes off. Over the centuries we had gotten 10 days behind. So we dropped ten days, but that didn't change the weekly cycle. People went to bed on Thursday, October 4 and woke up on Friday, October 15. The weekly cycle remained untouched.

Colossians 2:16

What about Colossians 2:16, where Paul says not to let anyone judge us concerning food, drink, a feast, new moon, and Sabbaths? Greek experts support a different translation of the text, which literally translated says, "Let not anyone judge you in food or drink or *in a part of* a feast or new moon or Sabbaths. These are a shadow of the things to come."

Using a triplet phrase common in the Old Testament (feast, new moon, and Sabbaths), Paul was alluding to any or all of eight Old Testament passages that referred to the *ceremonial sacrifices, which pointed to the Messiah*. He was telling his readers, as he does in so many other passages, that they didn't need to follow the Jewish ceremonial laws in order to be Christians. [14]

Where we are often confused is that the seventh-day Sabbath wasn't part of the Jewish ceremonial system pointing to the Messiah. It has always been a memorial of Creation.

The beauty of this corrected translation is that it makes this verse agree with all of Paul's other writings instead of forcing it to stand out all alone and exposed to criticism.

---

14. For deeper exegesis of this topic see Kim Papaioannou and Michael Mixolisi Sokupa, "Does Colossians 2:16 Abolish the Sabbath?" *Adventist Review*, February 23, 2012.

Keep any day

Some will say it's important that we keep a day but it doesn't matter which day, so long as we reserve one for God. After all, this commandment seems to be arbitrary, right? (It is not arbitrary, but for the sake of discussion, let's say it is.) However, we have already recalled another arbitrary test of loyalty in the very beginning—the tree of knowledge of good and evil. Would it have worked if Adam and Eve had said, "A tree is a tree. Just so long as we reserve one tree for God, that will be good enough." No, God arbitrarily specified a particular tree as a test of loyalty. With the seventh-day Sabbath, God has specified a particular day as a test of loyalty.

It's just not important

The argument we hear nowadays is simply that it's not important. But given what we have uncovered here in Revelation 14:7, it seems to be of particular importance in the last days of earth's history. It is the crux of deception. You simply can't interpret the final crisis in Revelation without this.

The mark of the beast is future

Understand, though, that we are not living in the final crisis right now. The mark of the beast doesn't yet exist. We are not being forced to make a choice between two worship days, as we will someday. So don't think that sincere Sunday-keeping Christians are bearing the mark of the beast today. That's not the case. Yes, we misunderstand, and, yes, we're misinformed, but we're not living in rebellion. God honors the sincerity of our hearts.

The question we must ask ourselves, though, is this: considering that judgment is going on right now, shouldn't we be following the best we know? If we know we are to keep the Sabbath holy and don't, will we not answer for that one day?

This business of obeying God's commandments, including the fourth one, is important. We would be unfaithful servants if we didn't tell it straight. We've just seen the strongest evidence that the Sabbath is the seal of God that opposes the mark of the beast at the end of time. The mark of the beast will be the counterfeit of the fourth commandment.

Investigate this in the Bible for yourself to find what is true. Anyone who is sincere in their search will not go wrong. Determine whether or not you are willing to follow the Lamb wherever He goes, and then dig into the Bible and see what you come up with.

Study Guide Outline

Chapter 13

1. Four ways we can fear God are by:

    a. Taking him _____

    b. Being in intimate _____ with him

    c. _____ him

    d. Avoiding _____.

2. Three ways we can give God glory are by:

    a. Making it clear who is doing the _____ in us

    b. Living a _____, vibrant life

    c. Being _____.

3. Revelation 14:7 is the center of the center of the center of the book of Revelation, and it strongly alludes to the first four _____ in Exodus.

4. The beast of Revelation 13 has a _____ of the first four commandments.

5. The fourth commandment is the _____ of God.

6. The counterfeit fourth commandment is the _____ of the beast.

Chapter 14

The Battle of Armageddon

Revelation 16

Our basic premise at the beginning was that Revelation is about Jesus Christ. Any interpretation we think we have discovered in Revelation that doesn't tell us something important about Jesus is suspect. We've heard many ideas about what Armageddon is, and most of them seem about as far away from teaching us something about Jesus as you can get.

Revelation 16 outlines a series of seven last plagues in earth's history. In Revelation the key to the battle of Armageddon begins in the sixth plague. Revelation 16:16 is the only verse where the word *Armageddon* appears in the Bible. To get a clear picture, we need to start in verse 12, where the sixth plague begins.

> The sixth angel poured out his bowl on the great river Euphrates, and its water was dried up to prepare the way for the kings from the East. Then I saw three evil spirits that looked like frogs; they came out of the mouth of the dragon, out of the mouth of the beast and out of the mouth of the false prophet. They are spirits of demons performing miraculous signs, and they go out to the kings of the whole world, to gather them for the battle on the great day of God Almighty.
>
> "Behold, I come like a thief! Blessed is he who stays awake and keeps his clothes with him, so that he may not go naked and be shamefully exposed."
>
> Then they gathered the kings together to the place that in Hebrew is called Armageddon (Revelation 16:12–16).

The other six plagues seem to occur worldwide, but this one appears to be limited to only the Euphrates River. It seems anti-climactic. Let's see what this is about using three different interpretation strategies.

First, we must examine the immediate and larger context of Revelation itself, because often the critical clues to understanding a passage in Revelation are located in another part of the book.

Second, as we know by now, it's important to understand the allusions that Revelation makes to the Old Testament. We will not understand Revelation if we don't know the Old Testament.

Finally, we must examine how other New Testament books handle the ideas we find in Revelation. John couldn't allude to specific New Testament books, but the ideas of the New Testament are obviously important in understanding the book of Revelation. The better you know your entire Bible, the better you understand Revelation.

As we try to understand the Euphrates River symbol, all three of these strategies will be useful.

When we begin to analyze a text, we should first notice the key ideas and key terms. Ask yourself, *what do I need to figure out in order to understand this passage?*

1. The sixth angel poured his bowl out into the great river Euphrates. *What is the great river Euphrates? What does that mean?*
2. Its water was dried up. *What is that all about?*
3. To prepare the way for kings from the east, or the rising of the sun. *Who are they?*

The first strategy, examining the larger context of Revelation, will eventually lead us to the answer to our first question concerning the great river Euphrates. Revelation itself explains what it is doing. The second strategy, searching for Old Testament allusions, will help us determine what the drying up of the Euphrates is all about. The third strategy, seeing how the New Testament handles the ideas, give us some perspective on the kings from the rising of the sun.

We don't have to guess about these interpretations. We can understand the battle of Armageddon from the Bible alone.

Question one

What is the great river Euphrates of Revelation 16:12? If we read further we find something interesting in Revelation 17:1. "One of the seven angels who had the seven bowls came and said to me, 'Come, I will show you the punishment of the great prostitute, who sits on many waters.' "

In vision, John had just finished seeing symbols, and now, as usual, it's time for some explanation. One of the angels who was pouring out one of the seven bowls on the earth says that he's going to explain to John the woman who sits on many waters. So this angel will explain one of the seven plagues, but we don't know which one. The only hint is that he's going to talk about the great prostitute who sits on many waters. Three of the plagues deal with water, so he must be explaining one of them. Is it the second, third, or sixth?

The unusual phrase "many waters" occurs elsewhere in the Bible. Many Bibles have a cross-reference to Jeremiah 51:13, because it includes the phrase, "You who live by many waters." This was a message to the people of Israel who were captives in Babylon. So the use of *many waters* in Revelation could be a reference to Babylon, which is a constant in the structure of Revelation. We will discover later what the symbol of Babylon represents at earth's final crisis.

Babylon was a twin city that straddled the Euphrates River. So this may be showing us that the *many waters* of Babylon may be the same as the Euphrates River. It's a clue to start with anyway, so let's confirm by looking at the prostitute who is sitting on these many waters.

Revelation 17:5 gives some information about her. It says her title is "Mystery, Babylon the great, the mother of prostitutes, and of the abominations of the earth." We're getting somewhere. The woman who sits on many waters is a prostitute named Babylon.

If the prostitute is the same as Babylon, then the *many waters* of Revelation 17 must be the Euphrates River. The Bible is in the process of interpreting itself.

We still don't know, however, what the Euphrates River represents. Some say the Euphrates River is the literal Euphrates River, and therefore this passage must be about the Middle East somehow. Others say no, the Euphrates River actually represents the entire area around the literal river, which is modern-day Iraq or the Middle East in general. Or maybe it's Middle Eastern oil because it flows like a river. Some suggest that it represents a person. Fortunately, the Bible makes it fairly clear.

After the little research we already did, we have enough information to see that Revelation clearly defines the symbol of the Euphrates River in Revelation 17:15. "Then the angel said to me, 'The waters you saw, where the prostitute sits, are . . . ' " It sounds like the angel is about to tell us what the many waters are, and, therefore, what the Euphrates represents. "The waters you saw, where the prostitute sits, are peoples, multitudes, nations and languages."

According to the Bible, is the Euphrates a literal river, or Iraq, or the Middle East, or Middle Eastern oil? No, none of the above. The Euphrates represents something much bigger than any of those things. According to the Bible, the Euphrates River represents the powers of earth, the people, multitudes, nations, and languages of our planet. We just tracked down the first answer using just the Bible.

Question two

What is the drying up of the Euphrates? How does one dry up people, multitudes, nations, and languages? This time, investigating an Old Testament allusion is going to help us. This mention of Babylon and the Euphrates recalls some Old Testament texts that describe the fall of Babylon and the drying up of the Euphrates River some 600 years before Revelation was written. If we want to understand what the Euphrates drying up means, that's where we're going to figure it out.

Reason 1: Oppressing God's people

> This is what the LORD Almighty says: "The people of Israel are oppressed, and the people of Judah as well. All their captors hold them fast, refusing to let them go. Yet their Redeemer is strong; the LORD Almighty is his name. He will vigorously defend their cause so that he may bring rest to their land, but unrest to those who live in Babylon" (Jeremiah 50:33–34).

The story here is that Babylon was oppressing God's people, and so God says that he will come to their defense. God wants Babylon to fall because of what it is doing to his people.

Tuck that idea up your sleeve for a minute and then notice the list here in the following verses.

> "A sword against the Babylonians!" declares the LORD— "against those who live in Babylon and against her officials and wise men! A sword against her false prophets!

They will become fools. A sword against her warriors! They will be filled with terror. A sword against her horses and chariots and all the foreigners in her ranks! They will become women. A sword against her treasures! They will be plundered" (Jeremiah 50:35–37).

What is God going to strike against in Babylon? It is her resources. What makes one nation greater than another is its resources: its leaders, its strategic thinkers, its religious leaders, its warriors, its weapons, its wealth, and so on. God will judge and strike at the heart of Babylon's greatness, which is her resources and the people who make her strong.

Now look at this: "A drought on her waters! They will dry up" (Jeremiah 50:38).

Long before Revelation was written, the Euphrates River was already a symbol of Babylon's greatness and protection. When Jeremiah says that the Euphrates dries up, it's all about Babylon and the fact that God casts judgment on her strength, resources, and defenses. John's hearers immediately recognized this. We have to work to see it. The more we immerse ourselves in the book of Revelation, the more we recognize language in the Old Testament.

Reason 2: Idol worshipers

Why was Babylon to fall? We already saw it was because she was oppressing the people of God, but verse 38 brings out another reason that fits into Revelation as well. Babylon was doomed to fall because the people were idol worshipers, "mad over fearsome idols." Revelation speaks a lot about those who worship images that are not God. They are idolaters. Again, the central issue in the battle of Armageddon is whom you worship.

"Therefore, this is what the LORD says: 'See, I will defend your cause and avenge you; I will dry up her sea and make her springs dry. Babylon will be a heap of ruins, a haunt of jackals, an object of horror and scorn, a place where no one lives' " (Jeremiah 51:36–37).

So God will avenge his people by drying up Babylon's waters. This is all Old Testament background concerning God's judgment on Babylon. When her resources are dried up, Babylon falls.

Reason 3: To rebuild Jerusalem

Isaiah 44:24–28 is another fall-of-Babylon passage. Watch for a third reason for God's judgment on Babylon.

> "This is what the LORD says—your Redeemer, who formed you in the womb: I am the LORD, who has made all things, who alone stretched out the heavens, who spread out the earth by myself, who foils the signs of false prophets and makes fools of diviners, who overthrows the learning of the wise and turns it into nonsense, who carries out the words of his servants and fulfills the predictions of his messengers, who says of Jerusalem, 'It shall be inhabited,' of the towns of Judah, 'They shall be built,' and of their ruins, 'I will restore them,' who says to the watery deep, 'Be dry, and I will dry up your streams,' who says of Cyrus, 'He is my shepherd and will accomplish all that I please; he will say of Jerusalem, "Let it be rebuilt," and of the temple, "Let its foundations be laid." ' "

Another of God's purposes for destroying Babylon is to make way for the rebuilding of Jerusalem. He wants Babylon to fall, first, because it oppresses God's people, second because it worships idols, and third because he wants to rebuild Jerusalem, which He finally does at the end of Revelation, when the New Jerusalem comes down out of heaven.

Keep in mind why we are interested in all this information about Babylon. We're investigating Armageddon, and that's exactly what we're reading about: the battle of Armageddon. The battle of Armageddon is the occasion when Babylon finally falls. The Bible interprets itself. You don't have to go outside of it to understand the story.

Often Revelation is interpreted as a simple vision of events that are happening or will happen on their own outside of God, but we're seeing something totally different here. Revelation is not just predicting events that are going to happen; it is revealing a picture of the God who is controlling events. He is active in the affairs of earth.

The book of Revelation is the revelation of Jesus Christ and the way he is controlling events that will lead to the eventual rescue of his people and the end of the war with Satan. God's purposes are so much bigger than just Iraq or Israel or the Middle East. The focus of the events of the end-time battle and Armageddon is God delivering his people.

The story behind the story

Cyrus is mentioned in Isaiah 44:28 because he was the leader who dried up the Euphrates on Belshazzar's last day as king of Babylon. The Babylonians were completely confident in the security of their city, and for good reason. They could withstand an indefinite siege because they could grow their own food inside the city and the Euphrates River ran right through the middle of the city, so they wouldn't run out of water.

Babylon's walls were 85 feet high. On top of the wall was enough room for a two-lane highway. Inside of that wall was a second 85-foot wall with another two-lane highway on it. If an attacker managed to get over the first wall he would find himself between two walls with people dropping rocks and boiling oil on him. There were also interior walls along the river itself, so if anyone tried to come into the city from the river, those gates would be shut and no one could get in that way.

Belshazzar was king, and Israel had been in Babylonian captivity for 70 years when Cyrus showed up with his army of Medes and Persians. Belshazzar was so confident in Cyrus' inability to capture the city that he staged a huge feast and didn't even bother to close the gates to the interior walls along the river.

During that feast, a hand appeared in mid-air and wrote some mysterious words on the wall. The prophet Daniel was called to interpret them, which he did. He informed Belshazzar that this was Babylon's last day.

Even as he spoke, Cyrus' army had diverted the Euphrates River, dried it up, marched under the wall, and entered the city through the open gates along the river.

Cyrus was God's agent of deliverance for his people. "This is what the LORD says to his anointed, to Cyrus, whose right hand I take hold of to subdue nations before him and to strip kings of their armor, to open doors before him so that gates will not be shut" (Isaiah 45:1).

God gave Cyrus the victory. Even so, God is still in control. He is directing the events leading up to the deliverance of his people.

Notice that Isaiah said, "This is what the LORD says to his *anointed*, to Cyrus, whose right hand I take hold of." Cyrus was a pagan king, but God calls him his anointed. "Anointed" in Hebrew is the word *messioch,* or messiah. God is speaking to his messiah—to Cyrus.

What is a pagan king doing with a title like that? God must be a bit more open-minded than we are. He has used some strange characters to accomplish his will throughout history. Think of Na'aman, the captain of an army known for its cruelty. Yet God called on him to become a believer in Assyria. Think of the Babylonian king Nebuchadnezzar. God turned him into a prophet, pagan though he was, and caused events to happen to him that turned him into a believer in the true God.

As God directs the events of history toward the deliverance of his people, he is able to use people we wouldn't expect. He called Cyrus his messiah, a title used for only one other person in all of Scripture: Jesus. Speaking to Cyrus, God said, "For the sake of Jacob my servant, of Israel my chosen, I summon you by name and bestow on you a title of honor, though you do not acknowledge me" (Isaiah 45:4). So Cyrus has an awesome role in the Old Testament. He is a type of Christ.

Kings from the rising of the sun

Why did God call Cyrus his messiah? Because Cyrus is the one who rescues God's oppressed people by drying up the Euphrates to conquer Babylon. Cyrus was a king from the east, the rising of the sun. Revelation 16:12 says that the Euphrates dries up to prepare the way for the kings from the rising of the sun.

The predictions of Isaiah and Jeremiah were written 100–150 years before Cyrus, and yet everything happened precisely the way it was foretold. God was in control then. He is in control now. He will be in control at the end, during the battle of Armageddon, when God sees to it that the resources of Babylon are dried up in order to rescue his people.

Please note where God's people are during the battle of Armageddon in the sixth plague. They are the ones being rescued, and therefore they are in Babylon. What does that tell you about some popular interpretations of the tribulation, in which God's people are taken away first? It doesn't work out that way when the Bible interprets itself.

With the people of God still inside the city of Babylon, Cyrus arrived, dried up the Euphrates, and marched under the river gates in the dry riverbed. God saw to it that the gates were wide open, and Cyrus took the city. Incredible story. Babylon was unconquerable, and Cyrus took it in one night.

The story of Armageddon

That is the story behind the story. It's the story of the battle of Armageddon. Armageddon is the story of an end-time Cyrus—Jesus Christ—who dries up an end-time Euphrates (the resources of Babylon) to conquer end-time Babylon, because he is delivering end-time Israel (God's remnant people), so that he can build a New Jerusalem (which we see in Revelation 21). That is what the battle of Armageddon is all about. That's what the last third of Revelation describes.

If we don't understand the Old Testament, we will never understand what is going on in these last chapters of Revelation. Once we understand the story behind the story, the battle of Armageddon becomes a lot easier to understand.

Question 3: Who are the kings from the rising of the sun?

Finally, let's figure out who are the kings from the rising of the sun. We will draw from some New Testament ideas to make sense of this symbol.

The phrase "rising of the sun" is used in two ways in the New Testament. It comes from the Greek word *anatoli*, which means "east." The New Testament uses this term many times in the context of direction, such as the wise men coming from the east. But the word is used in a second way. It's used to describe Jesus Christ.

In Luke 1:78 Zechariah sees a baby born, and when he gets his voice back, he sings a song in which he refers to Jesus. He calls him the *anatoli,* as a title or a name for Jesus. You don't see this as clearly in the English, but in the Greek it's the same word, used both for a direction and for Jesus.

So Jesus is somehow associated with the direction of the east in a special way. Matthew 24:27 tells how the coming of Jesus will be like lightning coming from the east to the west. It seems that Jesus will come from the *anatoli*, the east. In Revelation 7:2, John sees another angel coming up from the *anatoli* having the seal of the living God. This term *anatoli* is always used in the context of a positive power.

This is crucial because often people interpret these kings as a subset of what Revelation terms the "kings of the earth," who are enemies of God's people. But in fact this language is consistently used not for enemies of God's people but for Jesus Christ himself. It's never used in a negative sense.

"The sixth angel poured out his bowl on the great river Euphrates, and its water was dried up to prepare the way for the kings from the East"

(Revelation 16:12). The "kings from the rising of the sun" is a positive image and is clarified in Revelation 17:14. "They will make war against the Lamb, but the Lamb will overcome them because he is Lord of lords and King of kings—and with him will be his called, chosen and faithful followers."

Jesus isn't just the King; he is King over lots of kings. If Jesus is King of kings, who are the other kings?

"To him who loves us and has freed us from our sins by his blood, and has made us to be a kingdom and priests to serve his God and Father—to him be glory and power for ever and ever! Amen" (Revelation 1:5–6). The people of God are called kings and priests. Jesus arrives with his called, chosen, and faithful ones. These kings of the East are the forces of good, just as Cyrus came from the east and was a force of good for God's people. The power of God causes the drying up of the Euphrates, preparing the way for the rescue of his people—his called, chosen, and faithful. The kings of the East are Jesus and those with him who are rescuing his people.

We've answered our three original questions clearly, and we've done it with just the Bible.

Role of God's people in Armageddon

We have already seen how there are two sides to the final conflict: the side of evil waged by the dragon and his cohorts and the side of God's people. We know what the dragon and his allies are after, and we know the weapons they use. They want to destroy God's people through deception and violence. What, then, is the role of God's people in the battle of Armageddon? Are God's people using the same tactics as the forces of evil? Are sincere Christians being trained as army, air force, and marines? Does that fit into the picture of Jesus, gentle and humble, that we see in the Gospels? Does that fit with Jesus' command for us to love our enemies and do good to them that hate us?

Probably the clearest picture of Christians fighting a holy war is given in 2 Corinthians 10:3–4. "For though we live in the world, we do not wage war as the world does. The weapons we fight with are not the weapons of the world. On the contrary, they have divine power to demolish strongholds."

God's people don't wage war as the world does. The language is of war, but Christians don't fight as the world fights. Our weapons are not the weapons of the world, which are physical weapons designed to destroy people and strongholds.

In the battle of Armageddon, the forces of evil will use violence to coerce worship, but the forces of good will not. The weapons of God's people are clearly different. They use divine power to demolish strongholds. What kind of strongholds are they demolishing? "We demolish arguments and every pretension that sets itself up against the knowledge of God, and we take captive every thought to make it obedient to Christ" (2 Corinthians 10:5).

God's people are demolishing arguments, and things that stand against God, taking thoughts captive. The battle the people of God are engaged in is a battle for the mind. The battle of Armageddon is not primarily a military conflict; it is a spiritual war for people's minds and loyalty. Doesn't that make sense considering the great deception going on in the final conflict?

Considering that the dragon's primary tactic is deception and the struggle is for the loyalty and worship of the people of the world, it seems that the battle of Armageddon cannot be a literal, physical battle between two violent military powers. Rather, it's a symbolic war, and we know symbolism is default mode for Revelation.

During the spiritual battle of Armageddon, could literal war be happening at the same time? Probably, because it seems as though war is always going on somewhere in the world. It could even be major war. But that doesn't seem to be the battle of Armageddon itself. It cannot be, because God's people, the true Christians, do not fight a holy war with unholy methods.

New Testament battle language

This is a crucial concept. People have all sorts of ideas about the battle of Armageddon, that it's going to be a physical military battle between Russia or China and the US or Israel and Palestine, and so on. But physical war can only destroy the body, and Jesus tells us not to fear those who can destroy the body and not the soul. At the heart of the New Testament, the language of physical war is always a metaphor for spiritual war that's capable of destroying people's souls. Revelation is a New Testament book, and it should be understood in ways that are compatible with the rest of the New Testament. When the New Testament portrays battles, they are battles for peoples' hearts and minds.

We have already seen that when Revelation talks about Israel, it's speaking in a spiritual sense of God's true people. Israel in Revelation does not describe a physical nation, but a spiritual people. Physical nations fight physical battles. Spiritual people fight spiritual battles. If you wonder about that, just ask yourself if you have ever battled temptation. We constantly fight spiritual battles, and they are all too real.

We must be clear about the fact that the book of Revelation is using the language of war in exactly the same way that the rest of the New Testament does—in a spiritual way.

The heart of the battle of Armageddon

While the Old Testament often speaks of real military battles, we have seen that there is often a double meaning—a reason the story was told in the way it was. Cyrus's battle for Babylon was a real battle, but we saw how Cyrus is a type of Christ who battles spiritually for his people. While Babylon and the Euphrates were geographical locations, they symbolically represent the opponents of Christ and his church in the end time. This is spiritual language couched in physical metaphors.

Here is the heart of the battle of Armageddon, which should clinch any doubts about the spiritual nature of the war. Look again at the description of Armageddon in Revelation 16:13–16.

> Then I saw three evil spirits that looked like frogs; they came out of the mouth of the dragon, out of the mouth of the beast and out of the mouth of the false prophet. They are spirits of demons performing miraculous signs, and they go out to the kings of the whole world, to gather them for the battle on the great day of God Almighty. "Behold, I come like a thief! Blessed is he who stays awake and keeps his clothes with him, so that he may not go naked and be shamefully exposed." Then they gathered the kings together to the place that in Hebrew is called Armageddon.

This is clearly dealing with the battle of Armageddon in military language, so it's notable that verse 15 is included in the middle of it. "Behold, I come like a thief! Blessed is he who stays awake and keeps his clothes with him, so that he may not go naked and be shamefully exposed."

That language should sound familiar. It's the language of the gospel, the language of anticipation and spiritual preparation for the second coming of Jesus. It also parallels Revelation 3:17–20, which contains the same "thief, shame, nakedness, garments" language. It's an appeal to the church of Laodicea to receive the gold, the white robes, the eye salve so that its spiritual poverty may not be shamefully exposed.

First Thessalonians 5:1–11 talks about Jesus coming as a thief and the importance of staying awake, which is a spiritual metaphor. Matthew 24:42–44 is the parable of the 10 virgins and the importance of staying awake and being very observant as we approach the end of time. Right in the heart of the battle-of-Armageddon passage is a verse filled with the imagery of *spiritual* warfare.

This, in a nutshell, is what Armageddon really is: the climax of the final conflict in which spiritual deception is the dragon's primary strategy. And God's people resist him with the truth. That is the battle of Armageddon.

Study Guide Outline

Chapter 14

1. The key to the battle of Armageddon begins in the _____ plague.

2. If the prostitute is the same as Babylon, then the many waters of Revelation 17 must be the _____.

3. The Euphrates River represents _____ and _____ and _____ and _____.

4. Long before Revelation was written, the Euphrates River was already a symbol of Babylon's _____.

5. When Jeremiah says that the Euphrates dries up, it means God casting _____ on Babylon's strength, resources, and defenses.

6. When her resources are dried up, Babylon _____.

7. The battle of Armageddon is all about the fall of _____.

8. Cyrus is called _____ because he is the one who rescues God's oppressed people by drying up the Euphrates to conquer Babylon.

9. Cyrus is a symbol of _____.

10. The kings of the East are _____ and those with him rescuing his people.

11. The battle of Armageddon is not primarily a military conflict; it is a battle for the mind, a _____ war.

12. Armageddon is the climax of the final conflict in which _____ deception is the dragon's primary strategy.

Chapter 15

The Three Confederacies of Armageddon

Revelation 17

Revelation 17 is probably one of the toughest parts of the entire Bible to interpret, which makes it that much more intriguing to explore.

As we delve into Revelation 17 we will discover that three distinct worldwide confederacies emerge as participants in the end-time events. We can't address everything in the chapter, but we will see much that fits well into the thickening plot of the end-time conflict.

> One of the seven angels who had the seven bowls came and said to me, "Come, I will show you the punishment of the great prostitute, who sits on many waters. With her the kings of the earth committed adultery and the inhabitants of the earth were intoxicated with the wine of her adulteries."
>
> Then the angel carried me away in the Spirit into a desert. There I saw a woman sitting on a scarlet beast that was covered with blasphemous names and had seven heads and ten horns (Revelation 17:1–3).

With so many images, we start off bewildered at what it all means. We have angels, bowls, many waters, a prostitute and kings of the earth drunk on their immorality with her, a scarlet, seven-headed, ten-horned beast filled with blasphemous names, and so on. But as we have seen before, many of these symbols are just different names for the same things.

Vision versus explanation

Verse 1 tells about a great prostitute sitting on many waters, and verse

146

3 describes a woman on a scarlet beast. Are these two different women or the same one? We know that the kings and inhabitants of the earth in verse 2 are interacting with both the great prostitute (verse 1) and the woman (verse 3). The context alone leads us to believe the great prostitute and the woman are one and the same, but there's better evidence.

Note that John does not see the prostitute described in verse 1. The angel says he will show John the prostitute who sits on many waters, but John doesn't yet see her. He only hears about what he will see. Then in verse 3 the angel carries him away in the Spirit to see the prostitute he promised to show him. However, when John looks, he sees a woman sitting on a scarlet beast.

In apocalyptic style, the vision and the explanation of the vision are always two separate items. This is important enough for us to take a look at several examples.

In Daniel 2, the vision King Nebuchadnezzar saw was of an image of gold, silver, brass, iron, and clay. Later Daniel comes and explains the meaning of the vision. The vision was symbolic; the explanation was more literal. Daniel has a vision later on, in which he sees beasts and then hears the explanation from an angel. The vision is symbolic, the explanation more straightforward and literal.

In Revelation 5, John hears about the Lion of the tribe of Judah; however, when he looks, what he sees is a lamb that was slain. The Lion of the tribe of Judah that John heard about was the same thing as the lamb that he saw. Both the vision and the description represent Jesus by different names.

Another example is found in Revelation 7. John hears about 144,000, but he sees a great multitude that cannot be numbered.

In the book of Revelation, it's always this way. What John sees (vision) and what he hears (explanation) are always the same thing. Revelation 17:1, 2 has the explanation first and then the vision. The angel explains what John is about to see (a prostitute on many waters), and then he does in fact see it, but he sees it in the form of a woman riding on a scarlet beast. They are the same woman. A couple of verses later, we see that her name is Babylon.

More symbols

There are other images in this vision, such as many waters, kings of the earth, a scarlet beast. Are these different things or the same? These symbols also represent the same thing.

Don't confuse your beasts in Revelation. Sometimes we assume that just because the word *beast* is used, all beasts in Revelation are the same beast. It might be clearer if we used the word *animal* instead of beast because we expect different species of animals without assuming they are the same.

We already tracked down in the last chapter that the symbol of the many waters, the Euphrates River, represents the peoples and nations of the world who make Babylon strong. In other words, the powers of the world are what support Babylon, and when that support dries up, Babylon falls. The kings of the earth, naturally, lead the civil and political nations of the earth that support Babylon.

What about the scarlet beast? As we just noted, the angel told John he would see a prostitute sitting on many waters (peoples, languages, nations). What John actually saw was a woman riding on a scarlet beast. Thus the woman is also the prostitute, and the many waters is also the scarlet beast. The many waters, kings of the earth, inhabitants of the earth, scarlet beast—all of these symbols represent the same thing: the political powers of the world that support the prostitute Babylon. They are her resources.

The scarlet beast

Now look at Revelation 17:9–10. John gives us an important clue concerning the scarlet beast. "This calls for a mind with wisdom. The seven heads are seven hills on which the woman sits. They are also seven kings. Five have fallen, one is, the other has not yet come; but when he does come, he must remain for a little while."

This verse confirms what we are seeing: that a variety of symbols represent the same things. We're on target.

The heads of the scarlet beast are also hills and kings. The woman sits on many waters, which is also a scarlet beast, which is also seven hills, and seven kings. Ultimately what we are seeing in all these symbols is the secular, civil, political powers, the nations of the world coming together in an illicit relationship with this woman.

The woman

Who, then, is the woman receiving the support of the nations of the world?

> The woman was dressed in purple and scarlet, and was glittering with gold, precious stones and pearls. She held a golden cup in her hand, filled with abominable things and the filth of her adulteries. This title was written on her forehead: MYSTERY BABYLON THE GREAT THE MOTHER OF PROSTITUTES AND OF THE ABOMINATIONS OF THE EARTH (Revelation 17:4-5).

So this is Babylon, but we still don't know whom she represents. By now we know to look first for allusions. What parallels might we find in the Old Testament to a woman who looks like this? Most people think first of Jezebel, and she does fit in many ways. But there is something even more insidious that fits here: Israel's high priest. The woman of Revelation 17 is dressed in similar ways (purple and scarlet, gold, precious stones), and she is holding a cup (the high priest ministered with drink offerings), and most important, she had a title on her forehead, as did the high priest. His title read, "Holiness unto the Lord."

Many commentators have noted that the parallel to this woman is the strongest with Israel's high priest. That's not to say she is a high priest, but she is a counterfeit acting the part of high priest. She is on a spiritual mission.

Those familiar with the Old Testament know that the penalty for prostitution was stoning, with one exception. In the case of the daughter of a priest, she was to be burned (Leviticus 21:9). Later we see that this prostitute in Revelation is burned rather than stoned.

As we have already seen, Babylon isn't just any power. It's a counterfeit Christian power, and it's riding the scarlet beast. The scarlet beast represents the nations of the world, and the woman called Babylon who is riding them is a religious power. Spiritual powers are consorting with political powers—a union of church and state.

Adultery symbol

"With her the kings of the earth committed adultery and the inhabitants of the earth were intoxicated with the wine of her adulteries" (Revelation 17:2). This spiritual power and this secular power are committing adultery together. Since these are not two individuals, literal adultery is impossible. The spiritual group and the secular/political group hook up in an illicit relationship of some sort.

When two individuals come together in an extramarital relationship, the reason they become involved is usually that each of them is looking for something better than what they have. They have a common interest. They aren't happy the way it is at home, and they each believe that in this new relationship they are going to be better off together than they were apart.

Likewise, when the political world unites with spiritual Babylon, it's because they have a common interest and feel they will be better off together. They go into this relationship with eyes open, thinking that this is the best thing for the world and for them.

On the other hand, the inhabitants of the earth, those following the leaders, don't commit adultery. They get drunk, symbolically speaking. They go along because they are confused, intoxicated. They don't see clearly. The name Babylon itself means "confusion."

What will apparently happen in the last days is that the political powers of the world will find a reason to unite, and the religious powers of the world will also find a reason to unite, and for a while those two confederacies will come together with a common purpose. Revelation 17:14 hints at that purpose. It has something to do with the true people of God, because in the adulterous relationship the spiritual and political confederacies make war with the Lamb.

Three confederacies

We are still operating in the context of the final conflict and specifically the battle of Armageddon. By implication, that means there are three worldwide confederacies in the climax of the final conflict: a confederacy of false religion (Babylon), a confederacy of secular and political authority, and the third confederacy, made up of their enemies: God's last-day people on earth.

Fundamentally, there will be two sides in the conflict, because false religion and the political powers are united as one against the people of God. Three groups are involved, but two sides in the battle. The woman and the scarlet beast are against God and his people.

Confederacy of the saints

The confederacy of the saints will look different from the confederacy of religion. The confederacy of religion will be made up of the organized religions and religious institutions of the world, while possibly God's true people will not at this point be organized in institutional terms at all. Why not? Because, as mentioned earlier, running an institution requires money, and they won't be allowed to buy or sell.

Don't think this can't happen. Toss fear into the equation, and people will react in ways you would only think of in nightmares. When 9/11 happened, Americans were all too ready to throw away liberties in exchange for security. The scenario of Armageddon that we are beginning to see could happen quickly and easily when people are sufficiently afraid.

Revelation says that the combined religious and political powers will attack the people of God. Perhaps they blame them for whatever major disaster is facing the planet, similar to the way Roman emperor Nero blamed the Christians for the burning of Rome. God's people are on the run. They may no longer be organized institutionally but will be a spiritual movement that will exist in every nation, tribe, and language scattered throughout the world. They are united in a common faith and a common response to what is going on in the world.

United confederacies

Political powers tend toward disunity, but some great crisis must happen at the end of time that will cause the powers of the world to feel that unifying is their only hope for survival.

The same will likely happen with religions. A common cause will unite Catholics, Protestants, Muslims, Jews, Hindus, Buddhists, and others to create a confederacy of false religion. These religious entities will pull together, and the true people of God in those religions will begin to feel called out of them. "Come out of her [Babylon] my people" (Revelation 18:4).

That would mean, then, the people of God currently exist in every religion, including non-Christian ones. Is it possible that there are people of God in religions that don't even believe in God? Isn't it entirely reasonable to expect that the same God who bestows the title messiah on a pagan, idol-worshiping king would have people in pagan religions even today, whom he will call out at the time of the end?

Confirming the three confederacies

Here are the three confederacies in the final conflict. Consider all the different names by which they are called in Revelation.

Saints	Secular	Religious
Remnant	Kings of the earth	Babylon
144,000	Many waters	Great City
Great crowd	Earth dwellers	Prostitute
Kings of the east	Beast	Unholy trinity
Watchful	10 horns	Woman
Clothed	Cities of the nations	
Called	7 mountains	
Chosen	7 kings	
Faithful		

The Armageddon passage in Revelation 16 confirms these three groups.

1. **Confederacy of the saints**: In verse 12 are God's people in the battle of Armageddon symbolized by the kings from the rising of the sun, which represent Jesus and those allied with him.
2. **Religious confederacy**: In verse 13 are the dragon, beast, and false prophet, the driving power behind the confederacy of false religion.
3. **Political confederacy**: In verse 14 are the political powers represented by the Euphrates River and the kings of the earth.

The Scarlet Beast

Going back to Revelation 17, let's look at verses 12 and 13, since this concerns the three confederacies. "The ten horns you saw are ten kings who have not yet received a kingdom, but who for one hour will receive authority as kings along with the beast. They have one purpose and will give their power and authority to the beast."

This is the scarlet beast, which we know is also the kings of the earth, politically speaking. Its ten horns must be some subcategory of the kings of the earth, because they are the horns on the beast. So the scarlet beast represents all of the nations of the world collectively, but the ten horns are a subset of those who are given special power for the purpose of giving their power to the scarlet beast. When these ten kings give their power to the beast, this adulterous union becomes complete. So a major portion, if not all, of the world's nations are together going to throw in their lot with the religious power of Babylon, making this adulterous affair possible.

Naturally many people ask, who are these ten kings? We can't know yet, because they haven't appeared yet. But pay close attention when you see the major nations of the world unifying to help control major crises. Could it be the European Union, NATO, the G10 nations, the major economic powers of the world? The text says these ten nations have not been given their power yet, which seems to still be the case. We are not yet at the time of Armageddon, making it impossible to identify them. But they will receive their power at the right time for the purpose of uniting the world politically to be controlled by Babylon.

"The woman you saw is the great city that rules over the kings of the earth" (Revelation 17:18). The woman who is the great city Babylon rules over or controls the political powers of the world. That is what this union is all about. The nations of the world will unify and give their authority over to the control of the religious power, Babylon.

Summary

The frogs, which are the convincing messages of the counterfeit gospel of the false trinity, go out to gather the kings of the earth. They join the woman, who is false religion, and the people of the earth become drunk on this illicit union. To put it bluntly, at the end of time religious authority will come to dominate the world once again.

Don't think it can't happen. It happened in the past with the great empires of the world, with Nebuchadnezzar's Babylon being a perfect example. History shows that it has happened in Christian history as well. During the Middle Ages, the Christian church dominated even the political world with disastrous results. Religion was forced on people worldwide.

Battle of Armageddon: Final events

Here's the big picture of Armageddon: Two trinities will be at work: the holy and the unholy counterfeit. The unholy trinity is seeking the admiration and worship of the world, which only belongs to God. To do this, it deceives the people of earth. So in the plot of Revelation, there are two claims to godhead.

There are also two gospels. The counterfeit gospel is brought by the three evil spirits (Revelation 16:13–14), and the true gospel brought by the three angels (Revelation 14:6–12). Both of these are worldwide messages. Revelation reveals two claims to gospel truth.

The conflict is primarily spiritual. The real focus of the battle of Armageddon is a battle for the hearts and minds of the people. To whom will they give devotion and worship? More than likely, military conflict will continue and perhaps even escalate, but in the grand scheme of Revelation, any military conflicts would play a relatively minor role in the battle of Armageddon.

As these two rival gospels go out in power to the world, people divide more and more into two groups, following one gospel or the other. These messages being carried by the remnant and the counterfeit have become significant to the world. People from every nation, tribe, and language are paying attention. They are being forced to choose a side. Those who follow the genuine are God's people, and those who follow the counterfeit make up Babylon.

The true gospel going out and being accepted or rejected by each person will precipitate the formation of two confederacies: God's people (the bride of Christ, those who love the truth), and Babylon (the great prostitute, those who hate the truth)—but even though they hate the truth they will be "religious" and even Christian, so-called. These two sides will wage fierce spiritual war to persuade the secular middle to join them.

The secular middle

The secular middle is the truth-neutral people. Second Thessalonians 2 speaks of those who love the truth. Eventually, everyone will be forced to either love or hate the truth. But that's not the situation right now. The secular middle doesn't hate or love the truth. They are neutral. They don't have a strong opinion. They sit on the fence of the issue. They may have never even heard of the issue.

But when the gospel is preached, it's impossible to remain neutral. The preaching of the gospel causes people to either accept or reject the message. To ignore it is to be against it.

In the beginning, these two groups, the saints and Babylon, are trying to draw this middle group into their group as either lovers of truth or the haters of truth. It's obvious why those who love the truth would join God's people. They study things out and follow the truth no matter how unpopular it is. It's also obvious why haters of truth would join Babylon's side. They already want to believe the lie. But what would bring truth-neutral people into the camp of Babylon?

1. Deception and counterfeit convince them (Revelation 13 and Revelation 16:13–14). Near truth or apparent truth convinces them because it gives them an easy way to appease their consciences.

2. Fire from heaven and other signs convince them (Revelation 13:13–

14). Miracles convince people because they require that they see something to believe it. And if they do see it, they will believe it even if it's false.

3. The symbolic adultery or fornication of Revelation 17:2 convinces them (because adultery is all about compelling self-interest). The nations believe their life will be better in this illicit relationship.

4. Intoxication will convince them (Revelation 14:8; 17:2). The confusion of mob mentality has an intoxicating affect. They are caught up in the moment and aren't thinking.

The battle of Armageddon is a war for those who are not committed one way or the other. Some will go to God's people, and some to Babylon. The result of the battle of Armageddon is that only two groups emerge. The secular middle cannot remain neutral. God's people, the saints, are then sealed in their belief, and those who join Babylon are marked in their belief—or at least in their conformity.

The end

The way it ends is predicted in Revelation 17:16. "The beast and the ten horns you saw will hate the prostitute. They will bring her to ruin and leave her naked; they will eat her flesh and burn her with fire."

The beast and ten horns (political powers) will hate the prostitute (spiritual powers). This is a twist! They were united, but then the secular powers turn on the spiritual powers. The action of God isn't what destroys the counterfeit spiritual power. The political powers that supported her turn around and destroy her. Babylon meets her end through the political powers that supported her. The Euphrates dries up!

Apparently the deception comes unglued somehow. The political powers find out they have been deceived and they are angry. "For God has put it into their hearts to accomplish his purpose by agreeing to give the beast their power to rule, *until God's words are fulfilled*" (Revelation 17:17).

God is the one who puts them together, and God ultimately tears them apart. God is always in control of the events of this planet. As bad as things get, when God's purposes are fulfilled, the evil powers fall and tear each other part. The political powers change their minds. The affair is over.

The Old Testament story that Revelation alludes to here is the story of Amnon raping his sister and then hating her (2 Samuel 13). It is a metaphor for what happens between the nations of the world and Babylon.

What happens to the political powers? They are destroyed at the Second Coming, which occurs just after all of this violence (Revelation 19:17–21).

That is how Armageddon ends. The deception falls apart; the religious confederacy is destroyed by the political powers of earth; and Jesus returns.

The local perspective

Revelation sees all of this happening globally. But what is it going to look like locally? The details here, you understand, are only speculation, but after the amount of work we've done, it is educated speculation.

Imagine yourself as one of the saints. You are identified by your refusal to obey the counterfeit fourth commandment, which commands you to worship on a day other than the seventh-day Sabbath. As a result, you are not allowed to buy or sell. You are, for all practical purposes, cut off from society. If you have space you might plant a garden so you can eat. The grocery store is no longer an option.

In the meantime, your government, in cooperation with other countries of the world and a huge religious coalition, decides that all of the people who aren't obeying the ruling powers must be killed, or else God will not rescue the world from whatever great crisis it is in. A death decree is issued, and people come looking for you. When they find you, perhaps they discover you kneeling in prayer with the light of God shining around you, and maybe they even hear the voice of God (like in Isaiah 30:30) proclaim that you are one of his people. We don't know how the deception falls apart, but we have possible hints.

If indeed they suddenly hear the voice of God, what are the people carrying out the death decree going to think at that moment? *We've been deceived! We thought we were following God, and it turns out God is on the side of these outcasts.* They become furious at the religious leaders who duped them. They head back into town looking for the pastors and others who convinced them that God was on their side. Revelation does not give us all of these details clearly, but all the elements are there.

In the end, Babylon, this powerful religious confederacy, falls suddenly, and it is a great disappointment to many. Revelation 18 shows the anguish that comes to the nations and the people of the world as they see the fall of Babylon. They had hoped Babylon would bring them out of whatever catastrophe had frightened them so much.

So there we have, as best we can explain from the Bible alone, what Armageddon is all about. It's about separating the entire world into only two clearly delineated groups, one for and one against God. Those who love the truth and are willing to follow the Lamb wherever he goes, no matter how uncomfortable and no matter how unpopular, will come through on God's side of the battle, while those who hate the truth ultimately wind up on Satan's side of the battle.

If you have never made a firm decision about whether or not you love the truth and are ready and willing to follow the Lamb wherever he goes, now the time to do that. Understand that the Lamb nearly always operates in uncomfortable territory. He nearly always operates in the minority. The faithful never seem to be the large, popular group. Following Christ is by definition a path of difficulty in relation to the culture of the world and even the culture of established religion. Jesus himself was, after all, at odds with the religious leaders of his day.

Will you decide right now to follow the Lamb wherever He leads you?

Study Guide Outline

Chapter 15

1. Revelation 17 is probably one of the _____ parts of the Bible to understand.

2. What John sees (vision) and what he hears (explanation) is always the _____ thing in Revelation.

3. Many waters, kings of the earth, and the scarlet beast are _____ names for the same thing.

4. All these symbols represent a _____ of civil political powers.

5. The prostitute of Revelation 17 alludes to Israel's _____ _____.

6. Babylon may well represent a worldwide confederacy of _____, supported by the political powers of the world.

7. In the last days, the religions and the political powers of the world will find a reason to _____.

8. The three confederacies of Armageddon are:

   a. _____ confederacy

   b. _____ confederacy

   c. Confederacy of the _____

9. Babylon is the sum total of the _____ trinity.

10. At the end of time, religious authority will come to _____ the world once more.

11. Armageddon is primarily a _____ conflict.

12. The result of the battle of Armageddon is that two _____ emerge and no one can remain neutral.

13. Babylon meets her end through the _____ powers that supported her.

14. I choose now to love the truth, and I am willing to follow the Lamb wherever He goes. Yes or no. There's no middle ground.

Chapter 16

Sequence of Final Events

On the following page is Jon Paulien's 12-step sequence of events in chart form.

The gospel goes to the world

Step 1: The first thing that kicks off all of the final events is the gospel of Jesus Christ going to the entire world, as represented by the three angels of Revelation 14. God's people taking the gospel to every nation, tribe, language, and people triggers everything.

As Christians we are commanded to do this work of proclaiming the gospel, but it can be a discouraging thought. The population of earth is growing faster than we have been able to spread the gospel so far. But we have to remember that ultimately it is God who changes hearts. We aren't even called to convert people. That is Holy Spirit territory. Our commission, according to Matthew 28 is to go, teach, baptize, and make disciples. We are not called to have large churches. We are not called to be "successful" in ministry—at least not in the way we usually think of success. We are called to be faithful exactly where God has put us, and it is up to God to bring it all together. So we don't have to think on a huge scale in order to finish the work God has called us to do. We have to think small.

Every Christian should ask of themselves, *What would God have me do spiritually for the people immediately around me? Am I faithfully living and sharing the gospel right where I am? Am I myself learning how to live in an intimate relationship with Jesus Christ? Am I spending time in the Scripture and in prayer every single day, getting to know God better? Am I sharing with others what he is doing in my life?*

God will take care of making sure the gospel gets where it needs to go when his people are faithful in the local responsibilities he gives.

Jesus said in Matthew 24:14 that the proclamation of the gospel of the kingdom will go to the entire world and then the end will come. This message going to the world calls together the saints from every nation, language, and people.

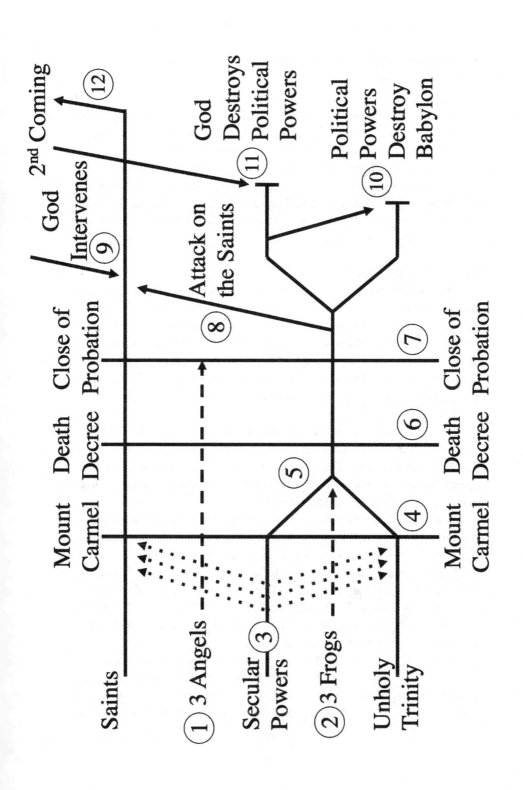

The counterfeit gospel goes to the world

Step 2: In reaction to the gospel going out to the world with Holy Spirit power, a counterfeit gospel that looks very close to the real thing also goes out to the whole world in similar power, represented by the three frogs who are counterfeits of the three angels. At the end of time, we will see two parallel versions of the gospel going to the world.

The true gospel spurs the saints to come together, and the counterfeit gospel spurs the formation of a confederacy of false religion led by the unholy trinity (Revelation 12, 13). This unholy trinity sends out the counterfeit three angels called the three frogs (Revelation 16:13–14) and calls the people to its version of the gospel.

Nations of earth unite

Step 3: The political powers of the world will also find a reason to unite. Revelation doesn't say exactly what precipitates this unification of political power, but in looking at the plagues of Revelation 16, one option could be an ecological disaster of some sort. All the water in the world being poisoned or the food supply being destroyed or climate change taking on new significance—any such scenario could trigger a fear reaction that causes the world to join politically for the sake of survival (Revelation 16:12; 17:1, 15).

Once these three groups have formed, there will be one final time of spiritual decision. The final proclamation of the gospel (Revelation 14:6–12; 18:4) goes out to the whole world and is challenged by the counterfeit gospel (Revelation 16:13–14). The two gospels struggle in a fierce spiritual battle for the loyalty of the secular middle.

The saints, through prayer and preaching, try to convince these uncommitted people to become loyal to God, while Babylon, or false religion, uses deception and miracles to bring the uncommitted to its side.

No one is allowed to remain in the middle, uncommitted, because when Babylon sees that people are still resisting her, she turns to coercion: economic sanctions and eventually a death decree (Revelation 13:15–17). The result is that the uncommitted are forced off the fence one direction or the other. Everyone must choose a side.

Second Thessalonians 2:10–12, speaking of the same time period in the future, says everyone will be deceived except those who love the truth. There will be those in the middle who at first are neutral, who neither love nor hate the truth, but they will be forced to choose to love the truth or to hate the truth, or at least to throw in their lot with those who hate the truth.

This is the purpose of Step 3: to bring everyone from the neutral middle to a commitment one way or the other. This is the final great conflict, the final battle for the hearts and souls of people, which eventually climaxes in the battle of Armageddon. In this spiritual battle, everyone's fate will be settled for eternity.

The order isn't clear

Understand that Revelation isn't perfectly clear on the order of these steps. There is some wiggle room. For instance, it's not stated which comes first, the religious or the political confederacy. They are ordered as 1, 2, and 3 in this book, but a 1-3-2 scenario is possible. We must remain flexible, remembering that the fulfillment of prophecy is nearly always different than we imagine it. We should expect things to look different than we imagine and not become overly confident in what we have imagined.

The 1-2-3 order of events is entirely possible because it seems from the perspective of the rest of the New Testament that the gospel going to the whole world is what starts the world on the fast track to the end. The world has been going for thousands of years without reaching the end, but one of these days it will finally reach a tipping point, and we'll be riding a sled that picks up speed quickly toward the second coming of Christ. The final events will be rapid ones. There's no way to know what "rapid" means in this context, but a year or two, maybe even less, for all of this to take place doesn't seem unreasonable.

Nations unite with false religion

Step 4: The secular powers begin to consider joining Babylon because of their mutual self-interest (the adultery image of Revelation 17:2). When Babylon reenacts the Mt. Carmel experience to prove that God is on its side by calling fire down from heaven in full view of men, enough people are convinced that the true God is on the side of Babylon, even though that is not actually the case (Revelation 13:13–14). Will this Mt. Carmel event look just like the story in Kings? Probably not.

Step 5: At this point the world's political powers hook up with the religious power (Revelation 16:12; 17:1, 3). This is the result of the battle of Armageddon. All public institutions, for all practical purposes, become a single entity (Babylon sitting on the scarlet beast or the woman on the Euphrates River). Religious power controls political power.

Saints threatened physically

Step 6: The world is completely unified except for the problematic saints who are resisting. Eventually the world realizes that there is a group of people not going along with what they think needs to happen for the good of everyone. The dragon is angry with the remnant. At some point the religio-political power singles out the saints and says, "It's better for one group to die than for the whole world to be destroyed." In other words, the powers will say, *"We have to do whatever it takes to destroy these people who are resisting us. God can't bless us as long as we allow these rebels to exist."*

As a result, God's true people are isolated and threatened. His people will have to go into hiding and survive under the death threats and economic sanctions.

Probation closes

Step 7: Human probation closes. That means that as far as heaven is concerned, everyone on earth has made his or her decision. Each person is either firmly committed to God or they are committed in some way to the enemies of God.

Again, we should remain flexible on the order of these steps. The close of probation could come at step five or six. It's not 100 percent clear in Revelation. But at some point around this time, probation closes (Revelation 10:7). Also, Revelation 15:5–8 shows that just before the bowl plagues are poured out, the temple in heaven ceases to function. "He that is righteous remains righteous. He that is filthy remains filthy." Everyone remains as they are from then on.

Saints are hunted

Step 8: The powers of the world then determine to carry out the destruction of God's people (Revelation 13:15 and Revelation 17:14) and everything appears lost for God's people. It looks as though they will be destroyed. They have lost everything, and their lives are under threat. It appears the unholy trinity will win.

God intervenes

Step 9: Whatever order we use for steps 5–8, we're clearly moving beyond that. In step 9 Christ intervenes on behalf of His people (Revelation 17:17), and they are miraculously delivered. The Euphrates River dries up (Revelation 16:12), the political powers turn on Babylon (Revelation 17:14, 16). Their unity splits apart. They become two separate entities again. The affair is over.

Nations destroy Babylon

Step 10: The nations destroy those who deceived them. Babylon falls at the hand of the powers she depended on, and God himself is part of the process (Revelation 17:16, 17). The end result is that both the secular powers and Babylon lose. However, the nations regret Babylon's demise even though she deceived them, because she was their last hope. Now everything is falling apart (Revelation 18:1–24).

That's what happens when you follow Satan. Things may look attractive now, but in the end it doesn't work.

The Second Coming

Step 11: At that point Jesus returns to earth and finishes the destruction of earth with 100-pound hail stones, massive earthquakes, mountains and islands being moved out of their places (Revelation 16:17–21). This all takes place at the Second Coming.

Revelation 19:17–21 also portrays the armies of heaven destroying the kings and powers of this earth with overwhelming power. The result is the complete stop to the advance of evil.

The saints go home

Step 12: Finally, Christ gathers the saints to be with him. Revelation 14:14–16 uses the metaphor of wheat harvest, while Revelation 19:6–16 has the metaphor of the gathering of the bride. The result is the saints joining Jesus in heavenly rest and peace.

There are 12 acts in the final events, as best we can make out based only on the Bible.

Study Guide Outline

Chapter 16

1. The 12 steps in the sequence of final events are:

   a. Step 1: The true _____ will go to the entire world.

   b. Step 2: The _____ gospel will go to the entire world.

   c. Step 3: Everyone must _____ between the true and the counterfeit.

   d. Step 4: Babylon convinces the world with _____ signs.

   e. Step 5: Babylon and the political powers _____.

   f. Step 6: The people of God are threatened with _____.

   g. Step 7: Probation _____.

   h. Step 8: The _____ are attacked.

   i. Step 9: God miraculously _____ on behalf of the saints.

   j. Step 10: The political powers _____ Babylon.

   k. Step 11: The _____ powers are destroyed at the Second Coming.

   l. Step 12: God's people go to meet the Lord in the _____.

2. Imagining the future is dangerous if we are too _____ in our imagination.

Chapter 17

How to Recognize the Second Coming

Imagine waking up one morning and flipping on CNN to catch the news, and as you're switching channels you notice that all of them are showing the same thing. The media is obviously captivated by a man whom you must admit is pretty incredible. Maybe he is wearing white robes, maybe he looks a lot like the portraits of Jesus we see everywhere—only, unlike the pictures, this man has a glow about him that is other-earthly. Your heart leaps. Something incredible is happening.

The entire world is mesmerized as this man compassionately heals the sick and charismatically preaches that the kingdom of heaven has come. He appears to prove from the Bible that this is the way it was intended to be from the beginning. And his arguments are persuasive. It sounds like Bible truth. But still, in the back of your mind is a nagging suspicion. Something doesn't seem right, in spite of what your eyes and ears are telling you.

We have worked through a lot of material in Revelation, discerning a diabolical deception in the works that will be so close a counterfeit to the truth that even God's people will tremble at its persuasiveness.

Revelation gives a general picture of the nature of this grand deception, but it does not fill in all of the details. Much is left to imagination, which is dangerous territory when it comes to the future because much, even most, of our imagination concerning the future is nothing more than speculation. The Bible is fairly limited in the details it gives concerning the future. Prophecy operates in broad strokes rather than fine detail.

The scenario of seeing someone on CNN may happen like that someday, but more than likely it won't. The final great deception described in Revelation will be so convincing that even God's spiritually well-grounded people could be deceived if God were to allow that.

God's people will not see through this deception because they have correctly imagined the future while others have imagined it incorrectly. We can easily become over-confident in the way we imagine future events will play out. The impression I get from what Jesus said is that no one really understands what the counterfeit return of Christ is going to look like in sufficient detail to recognize it. The Bible has never given us that much information on the subject.

What Jesus did tell us in a lot of detail is what his real coming will look like, so that we will recognize that. However, generally speaking, people remain unclear in their understanding of the manner of Christ's coming, in spite of all the information we've been given.

Gospel goes to the entire world

There are some prerequisites that must take place before Jesus will return. Certain things must occur. He mentions wars, rumors of wars, natural disasters, and so on, but he says these are not the signs of his return; they are only "labor pains." They are the early contractions and not signs of imminent birth. So don't pay attention to these things as specific signs.

The major sign that his coming is about to happen is that the gospel will go to the entire world. "This gospel of the kingdom will be preached in the whole world as a testimony to all nations, and then the end will come" (Matthew 24:14).

We could argue that this gospel has already gone to the world, at least by satellite TV or the Internet, if not in person. However, we have seen that the gospel going to the entire world means that the world will pay full attention to it and will react to it. It will be significant to the world, whereas right now the gospel is insignificant to a huge portion of the world's population.

It will be unexpected

Jesus also points out that life will go on as usual for most people. Even though the people of God will recognize signs of the end, others will not. It will be life as usual—eating, drinking, and marrying. "For in the days before the flood, people were eating and drinking, marrying and giving in marriage, up to the day Noah entered the ark" (Matthew 24:38).

Jesus' coming will not be expected by most people. We don't know exactly what the counterfeit second coming is going to look like, but if there happens to be any sort of announcement concerning this false coming, we can know something is wrong. In other words, if the world as a whole happens to be looking for Jesus at a particular time, be suspicious. "Now, brothers, about times and dates we do not need to write to you, for you know very well that the day of the Lord will come like a thief in the night" (1 Thessalonians 5:1–2).

Here's another thief-in-the-night passage: "Understand this: If the owner of the house had known at what time of night the thief was coming, he would have kept watch and would not have let his house be broken into. So you also must be ready, because the Son of Man will come at an hour when you do not expect him" (Matthew 24:43–44).

Perhaps the reason people won't expect the real return of Christ will have something to do with the fact that they think he has already come. They have been deceived by a false Christ. After all, who expects their guest to arrive when their guest has already arrived?

According to 1 Thessalonians 5:4, for those who walk in the light of the day, Jesus' coming won't be unexpected. "But you, brothers, are not in darkness so that this day should surprise you like a thief." Just as Noah expected the flood while no one else did, God's people will recognize the significant events happening around them, which most everyone else will not recognize. For the majority of earth's inhabitants, Jesus will come as a thief in the night, not because he sneaks in quietly but because he is not expected.

Impersonators

According to Matthew 24:24, just before the real coming of Christ we should expect false Christs and false prophets to appear. Now this has been happening to some degree ever since Jesus left the first time. But the impersonators haven't been very convincing. Jesus seems to indicate that some very convincing impersonators will show up just before his return. "For false Christs and false prophets will appear and perform great signs and miracles to deceive even the elect—if that were possible" (Matthew 24:24).

When these false impersonators come, the inhabitants of the earth will sit up and take note because these counterfeits shouldn't be able to do what they are doing. They will be performing miraculous signs that only God should be able to do. God's people must be on the lookout for astounding miracles before the Second Coming that, these people claim, are the result of Jesus' second coming. There are true miracles, but miracles that claim to be the result of the Second Coming must be suspect.

Tribulation

Here's another sign:

> Immediately after the distress of those days "the sun
> will be darkened, and the moon will not give its light; the
> stars will fall from the sky, and the heavenly bodies will
> be shaken." At that time the sign of the Son of Man will
> appear in the sky, and all the nations of the earth will
> mourn. They will see the Son of Man coming on the
> clouds of the sky, with power and great glory (Matthew
> 24:29–30).

The parallel to the end-time tribulation is the Israelites in Egypt just
before the exodus. God's people were in the thick of the plagues, but they
were protected. After the time of tribulation, there will be some signs in
the heavens of the sun and moon darkening and the stars falling. Some
of these signs have already happened, but it seems likely they will happen
again immediately before Jesus returns.

If we're ever tempted to believe that Jesus has returned and these
signs have not occurred, we have reason to suspect a false Christ.

These are all precursors to the return of Christ.

The cloud

Now let's look at the event itself and what that will look like. "At that
time the sign of the Son of Man will appear in the sky, and all the nations
of the earth will mourn. They will see the Son of Man coming on the
clouds of the sky, with power and great glory" (Matthew 24:30).

He will come on the clouds of the sky. At Jesus' ascension in Acts
1:11, he was lifted up as they looked on, and a cloud received him out of
their sight. Then angels informed the people that Jesus would come back
just as they had seen him go. He will come in the clouds as we watch.

Every eye

Revelation 1:7 says the same thing as Matthew 24 and adds a detail.
"Look, he is coming with the clouds, and every eye will see him, even those
who pierced him."

He will come in the clouds, and every eye will see him. He will be
seen in person, not on TV or Internet streaming. If you do not see Jesus

coming in the clouds for yourself, do not believe reports of the Second Coming no matter how much of a biblical case is made for it.

No one is unconvinced

"For as lightning that comes from the east is visible even in the west, so will be the coming of the Son of Man" (Matthew 24:27). At the counterfeit return of Christ, the redeemed will be unconvinced. At the real Second Coming there will be no doubt in anyone's mind as to what is happening. If someone claims the Second Coming has happened and anyone is unconvinced, then the Second Coming has not happened.

Company

Jude 14 tell us that Jesus will be coming with thousands of his holy ones. He won't be alone or have a small entourage; he will be accompanied by a mighty host of beings. We don't know what the counterfeit second coming will look like, but this is something to keep in mind for recognizing the real Second Coming.

Noise

Jesus' coming will also be noisy. "For the Lord himself will come down from heaven, with a loud command, with the voice of the archangel and with the trumpet call of God, and the dead in Christ will rise first" (1 Thessalonians 4:16).

Jesus' coming is going to be a noisy, spectacular display in the sky.

Resurrection

The effect of that noisy trumpet blast, according to that verse, is that the cemeteries will be ripped apart and the dead in Christ will arise—a massive resurrection. If someone says that the Second Coming has happened, just glance out at the nearest cemetery and you will know that that cannot be. Well, unless, of course, counterfeit performers of miracles are able to pull off a stunt like that. Could that really happen? Don't be overly sure. Just add this to your knowledge base of what will accompany the real return of Christ.

Transformation

If you're looking for confirmation of the real Second Coming, you won't even have to seek out the nearest cemetery—at least, not if you are one of the redeemed. Because 1 Corinthians 15 tells us something else is going to happen at the sounding of that trumpet. "Listen, I tell you a mystery: We will not all sleep, but we will all be changed—in a flash, in the twinkling of an eye, at the last trumpet. For the trumpet will sound, the dead will be raised imperishable, and we will be changed" (1 Corinthians 15:51–52).

At the Second Coming, as soon as you hear the trumpet, you will instantly change physically and mentally. You will know!

Our reaction

Isaiah 25:9 tells us something else that will happen as we see and hear this grand display in the sky. The redeemed of God are going to say something together:

"In that day they will say, 'Surely this is our God; we trusted in him, and he saved us. This is the LORD, we trusted in him; let us rejoice and be glad in his salvation.' "

Judgment

Matthew 16:27 tells us something else that will happen at the second coming. "For the Son of Man is going to come in his Father's glory with his angels, and then he will reward each person according to what he has done."

At the Second Coming there will be a judgment.

Destruction

Jesus' coming will be accompanied by massive destruction. "While people are saying, 'Peace and safety,' destruction will come on them suddenly, as labor pains on a pregnant woman, and they will not escape" (1 Thessalonians 5:3).

Those claiming peace and safety will be destroyed at the Second Coming.

Rapture

Finally, 1 Thessalonians 4:17 describes what will happen with the redeemed at the Second Coming. "After that, we who are still alive and are left will be caught up together with them in the clouds to meet the Lord in the air. And so we will be with the Lord forever."

If you hear that the Second Coming has happened and your feet don't leave the ground to meet the One (Jesus) whose feet aren't going to touch the ground, then you're either not going or you've got the wrong Second Coming.

Beware the counterfeit

False Christs will come. False prophets will come. Jesus said so. We're going to hear a believable story that Jesus has come back to earth the second time in a way that we did not see him go. We may be told that he came secretly and quietly. Satan is already engineering a counterfeit second coming that he is going to support by saying, "It is written." But he will not be allowed to counterfeit the precise manner of Jesus' coming the way Jesus described it. If we will only avail ourselves of it, we have enough information about the genuine to detect the counterfeit.

God has given numerous safety stops to keep us from believing the lie. Don't spend your time trying to figure out exactly what the deception is going to look like. Whatever you think of, it won't be like that.

Time and again throughout history, people have thought they had a clear picture of the way prophecy would be fulfilled, and in every instance it's different than they expect. The only things we can depend on are the clear signs that Jesus gave us.

"I have told you everything in advance," said Jesus in Matthew 24. We have no reason to be deceived by the counterfeit when it comes, no matter how convincing it may be, if we keep our eyes fixed on Jesus and pay attention to his word to us.

You can find more resources from Jeff Scoggins at www.scoggins.biz

Study Guide Outline

Chapter 17

1. Signs of Jesus' return:

    a. The gospel goes out in a way _____ to the world (Matt. 24:14).

    b. Most people will not _____ Jesus' return when it happens (Matt. 24:38, 1 Thess. 5:1, 2).

    c. False impersonators working _____ will claim to be Jesus (Matt. 24:24).

    d. After the tribulation, the sun and moon will be _____ and the stars will fall just before Jesus arrives (Matt. 24:29, 30).

2. The actual Second Coming:

    a. Jesus will come in the _____ (Matt. 24:30).

    b. Everyone on earth will actually _____ Jesus come (Rev. 1:7).

    c. Jesus' coming will be like _____ flashing from the east to the west (Matt. 24:27) and no one will be _____ of the reality of it.

    d. Jesus will be _____ by thousands and thousands of beings (Jude 14).

    e. The Second Coming will be _____ (1 Thess. 4:16).

    f. The Second Coming will be marked by a massive _____ of the redeemed (1 Thess. 4:16).

    g. At the trumpet blast, the redeemed will be instantly _____ physically and mentally (1 Cor. 15:51, 52).

h. The redeemed will _____ Isaiah 29:5 together.

i. The Second Coming will include _____ (Matthew 16:27).

j. The Second Coming will be accompanied by _____ (1 Thess. 5:3).

k. The _____ will be caught up to meet Jesus in the air (1 Thess. 4:17).

3. Do not concentrate on what the _____ might look like; concentrate on what the real thing will be like.

Appendix

Detecting Allusions

Detecting allusions is important in understanding Revelation, because John would have assumed that his readers would understand a big picture by the mention of a single word or phrase. When we don't have that past history, we are missing a significant piece of what we need in order to understand. So we must learn how to detect allusions. The basic method is to find parallels with other scriptures that don't seem to be co-incidental. It takes work, but the reward is worth it.

After we have become familiar with the overall idea of the passage we're investigating, and after we understand as best we can the key words, and after we have compared translations and paid attention to word relationships, finally we can begin to look for allusions.

Verbal parallels

We begin to find allusions by looking for verbal parallels. For example, with the fifth seal in Revelation 6:9–11, the passage says, "When he opened the fifth seal, I saw under the altar the souls of those who had been slain because of the word of God and the testimony they had maintained. They called out in a loud voice, 'How long, Sovereign Lord, holy and true, until you judge the inhabitants of the earth and avenge our blood?' Then each of them was given a white robe, and they were told to wait a little longer, until the number of their fellow servants and brothers who were to be killed as they had been was completed."

To understand this passage, the first thing we must do is to determine the verbal parallels it has with other scriptures. We do that by picking out the important words to compare. We can skip unimportant words like *and* and *the*. We can mark the major words by highlighting them. A computer is handy for this, because highlighting is easy and can be tagged in different colors and changed if necessary. You probably shouldn't do this directly in your Bible, because it will be a mess before you're done.

First, identify the important words, and compare these words with other scriptures to see what lines up.

> When he opened the fifth seal, I saw under the altar the souls of those who had been slain because of the word of God and the testimony they had maintained. They called out in a loud voice, "How long, Sovereign Lord, holy and true, until you judge the inhabitants of the earth and avenge our blood?" Then each of them was given a white robe, and they were told to wait a little longer, until the number of their fellow servants and brothers who were to be killed as they had been was completed.

It's good to research these words a little. For instance, this version says, "wait a little longer," whereas other versions say, "rest a little longer." That may or may not be significant, but it's good to be aware of the differences so that you can think it through.

Grab a lexicon or your Bible software and look up the word to see the dictionary definition because it's helpful to understand the range of meaning that a word can carry. For instance, the word *slain* can be a verb or a noun referring to the act of being killed or it can describe someone who has already been killed. These differences might affect the end result of your research.

Parallels in Revelation

Once we have identified the key words that we will compare, we should investigate the possible parallels within Revelation itself, because the more clues we can gain from John in the book of Revelation, the more sure we can be of his intentions.

First note where this passage fits in the chiastic structure (see chapter 5 of this book). Then take the major words in the passage and compare them with other parts of Revelation. A computer is extremely helpful for this work because of its search capabilities. A good concordance can help you do the same thing; it just takes longer. For example, search for the word *altar* in Revelation and set all the verses you find to one side. Then take the next word *slain* and do the same thing, and the same with each of the major words in the passage you're investigating.

Next take all the verses your cross-referencing uncovered and highlight in those passages all of the key words you highlighted in your original passage. Many of the verses may have multiple words that are the same in both passages. The more words you find in common with the passage you are investigating, the stronger case you have for a parallel passage.

If you have two unique words in both passages, you have a possible parallel and the more unique words you find, the stronger the likelihood of an intended allusion. One of the strongest allusions identified in the Bible has about eight words in common. If you get 15 or 20 words in common, the author is more likely quoting than alluding.

So in our search we discover that Revelation 1:9 has three words/phrases that are the same as Revelation 6:9–11: *brother, word of God,* and *testimony of Jesus.* Revelation 1:9 says, "I, John, your <u>brother</u> and companion in the suffering and kingdom and patient endurance that are ours in Jesus, was on the island of Patmos because of the <u>word of God</u> and the <u>testimony of Jesus</u>."

There is likely a connection between that verse and Revelation 6:9–11. It's definitely something to look into further.

We also find that Revelation 7:9–14 has five words in common with our passage, and so on. What we have left after this comparison, hopefully, is a passage or two that seem to have a lot in common with the one we're investigating.

Now as we take those passages together, we start to see a broader picture emerging.

Thematic parallels

Next we want to crystallize the picture a bit more, and we can do that by looking at the thematic parallels between our verses. When reading for verbal parallels, it was pretty basic to look for the same word. Now we have to think a little more creatively to see if they have themes that overlap. For instance, are there themes of judgment or war or persecution or something else?

We found that Revelation 1:9 had three verbal parallels (single underline):

"I John, who also am your <u>brother</u>, and <u>companion</u> in <u>tribulation</u>, and in the kingdom and patience of Jesus Christ, was in the isle that is called Patmos, for the <u>word of God,</u> and for the <u>testimony of Jesus</u> Christ."

We notice that the word *tribulation* sounds like a theme of the souls under the altar who were *persecuted.* Here is a theme of suffering. So we mark that in a different color (double underline). We have discovered a common theme between our two passages.

We also see the word *companion.* The souls under the altar are told to wait a little longer until their *fellow servants* join them. There's another theme that strengthens the connection between these two passages: both passage are concerned with other believers in service with those who are suffering.

By now we are becoming fairly confident that there is some valuable information here that can help us better understand the passage of the souls under the altar. We can also see where the critical eye of our peers can be valuable. We don't want to see connections where there are none, so it's good to run our findings by others who are knowledgeable in the method we are using. This is a commonly accepted method among scholars, so we should be able to find people to bounce our findings off of, even if we're doing it though respected commentaries or similar resources.

Figuring it out

Once we have established that we do in fact see a real connection between these passages, we get into the investigative/detective part. It's fun. We get to see what extra information we gain from this passage about the other passage we are investigating. For example, John calls *himself* a brother and companion to those who are suffering under the altar. He is one of the brothers.

Right away that tells us something about the souls under the altar: they can't just be a specific group of martyrs already dead. They must be a broader group than we might assume from reading this passage in isolation. Apparently, John sees these souls under the altar as those who are suffering for Christ, not just those who are already dead, because he is one of them and he isn't dead. That is an interesting bit of information we just gathered by putting two and two together using a hermeneutically sound method. It's as scientific as you can get with Bible study.

After we have done this research with the first verse, we go on to the next and the next, and all the time we are building interconnectedness within the framework of the Bible. One passage gives additional information that then connects it to another and soon our picture becomes clearer.

The word *tribulation* in Revelation 1:9 clued us into some major thematic parallels in Revelation 2:8–11. The common words and themes lead us to more information in Revelation 3, 7, 8, 11, 12, 14, 16, 17, 18, 19, 20, and 22. Putting everything together:

1. We learn more about the saints under the altar in the letters to the churches of Philadelphia and Smyrna.
2. We learn that the inhabitants of earth are the same as those described

as "those who claim to be Jews but are not but are of the synagogue of Satan."

3. We learn that he who overcomes is the same group as those whose names are written in the book of life.

4. We learn that the inhabitants of earth will eventually acknowledge they were wrong and that God will have the persecutors fall at the feet of the saints.

5. We learn that keeping the saints from the hour of temptation is likely equated with resting for a little while.

6. We learn that the souls under the altar are very likely the same as the 144,000, which are also the same as the great multitude that can't be numbered.

We could go on with what we have learned just from investigating the three verses of Revelation 6:9–11. It is work, but the results can be astounding.

We found parallels within Revelation, but we can use the same method for finding John's allusions in the Old Testament as well. The only difference is that since we aren't working with material that John wrote, we add a step to help determine whether or not John really intended the allusion we think we see or not. We must classify the parallel Old Testament passages.

1. **Non-allusions.** In searching for verbal parallels we will find parallels in words that can easily be classified as non-allusions. We can be pretty sure that Revelation doesn't have this passage in mind, even though some words are the same.

2. **Possible allusions.** Some will be classified as possible allusions. There is the potential Revelation could have this Old Testament passage in mind, but there isn't enough evidence to be sure.

3. **Probable allusions.** Then there will be a few passages that will come to the surface as probable allusions. There are enough parallel words and themes that it's likely Revelation is alluding to this passage.

4. **Certain allusions.** Finally, one or maybe two passages may surface as certain allusions based on the evidence.

Since we already did the work on Revelation 6:9–11, here is one Old Testament allusion that seems to sift to the top.

The LORD will judge his people and have compassion on

his servants when he sees their strength is gone and no one is left, slave or free. He will say: "Now where are their gods, the rock they took refuge in, the gods who ate the fat of their sacrifices and drank the wine of their drink offerings? Let them rise up to help you! Let them give you shelter! See now that I myself am He! There is no god besides me. I put to death and I bring to life, I have wounded and I will heal, and no one can deliver out of my hand. I lift my hand to heaven and declare: As surely as I live forever, when I sharpen my flashing sword and my hand grasps it in judgment, I will take vengeance on my adversaries and repay those who hate me. I will make my arrows drunk with blood, while my sword devours flesh: the blood of the slain and the captives, the heads of the enemy leaders." Rejoice, O nations, with his people, for he will avenge the blood of his servants; he will take vengeance on his enemies and make atonement for his land and people (Deuteronomy 32:36).

Summary of symbols

Altar: We learn that the altar is a powerful image, and in the broader context of Revelation it is most notably a symbol of worshiping the true God.

Prayer: We find that it is the prayers of the saints that bring on the final events of earth's history.

Cross: We find that although they are saints, they are not completely innocent of all wrongdoing. They must rest "under" the sacrifice of Christ until they are given the perfect righteousness of Christ. As usual, John brings the cross of Jesus into the picture.

Souls that were slain: We learn that these are the saints who have suffered and/or died while they were faithful to God, and we discover that this group is also known by other names throughout Revelation.

Word of God: We discover that the obedience of the saints to the word of God symbolizes obedience to the covenant, which includes the Scriptures with both the law and the prophets, accepting the gospel message as it is in Jesus with his death and resurrection, and acknowledging God the creator.

Testimony: We learn that this symbolizes obedience to the covenant by being an authentic witness, keeping the Ten Commandments, accepting the spirit of prophecy, sharing the faith, and worshiping God. *Word of God* and *testimony* is remnant people language, which opens up a huge realm to explore further.

Avenge our blood: This is God's retribution upon the wicked for their sins and mistreatment of his people.

Inhabitants of earth: This symbolizes those whom God will punish for their wickedness. This group is also known by other names throughout Revelation.

White robes: This symbolizes Christ's covering righteousness for his people.

To even begin to understand any part of Revelation, we must become intimately knowledgeable of the entire story of Revelation and how the Old Testament and the fulfillment of the Messianic prophecies broadens the picture we find in Revelation.

Happy working!

Study Guide Answer Key

Chapter 1
1. In Stage One we will lay a <u>foundation</u> for seeing the underlying story of Revelation.
2. In Stage Two we will use our particular <u>method</u> of Bible study to begin making sense of the text.
3. In Stage Three we will paint the big picture and see a flow chart of the <u>sequence</u> of events at the end of the world.

Chapter 2
1. We need a sound method of interpreting prophecy.
2. The Bible <u>interprets</u> its own symbols.
3. Prophecy is clear in <u>hindsight</u> but fuzzy when it points to the future.

Chapter 3
1. The reason the book of Revelation has bad <u>grammar</u> is that on Patmos, John had no access to an editor.
2. Five limitations of biblical authority are:
   a. <u>Accommodation</u> to the human situation
   b. The Bible doesn't answer every <u>question</u>
   c. Bible stories that are open to varieties of <u>interpretation</u>
   d. The temptation to try to make the Bible defend what we already <u>believe</u>
   e. We should approach the Bible with a great deal of <u>humility</u> because we are limited in our understanding.
3. God speaks to his prophets in their own <u>language</u> and time in ways the prophet will understand.
4. God <u>limits</u> himself by coming down to our level.
5. God's <u>intent</u> for prophecy comes through even if the prophet doesn't understand that part of it.
6. Safe ways to approach the Bible:
   a. Come with <u>prayer</u> and self-distrust
   b. Use <u>multiple</u> translations
   c. Give <u>clear</u> texts the priority
   d. Give general <u>reading</u> higher priority than study
   e. Study with <u>others</u>.

Chapter 4

1. Method for interpreting prophecy:
   a. Read <u>lightly</u> and broadly.
   b. Read the passage <u>intensively</u>.
   c. Compare <u>translations</u>.
   d. Consider <u>word</u> relationships.
   e. Pay careful attention to the Old Testament <u>background</u>.
   f. Try to understand how the Old Testament imagery is <u>transformed</u> by the gospel.
2. It's vital to understand the structure of Revelation in order to interpret it well.
   a. In a chiastic structure, the decisive portion is at the <u>center</u> of the book.
   b. Some verses of Revelation point both <u>forward</u> and backward.
   c. Allusion is employed to direct a reader's mind to a larger <u>context/story</u> using just a word or phrase as a reminder.
   d. John alludes to the Old Testament <u>many</u> times in Revelation.

Chapter 5

1. Being able to detect <u>allusions</u> in Revelation is critical to interpreting the book.
2. First try to detect allusions within Revelation by searching for <u>verbal</u> parallels.
3. Next, try to detect allusions in the Old Testament by searching for <u>verbal</u> parallels.
4. Next, search for <u>thematic</u> parallels.
5. Finally, search for <u>structural</u> parallels.

Chapter 6

1. Revelation is about <u>Jesus</u>.
2. Jesus became the new Adam in order to become the new <u>representative</u> of the human race.
3. Even though Jesus relived Adam's life perfectly, he still accepted the <u>consequences</u> of Adam's failure.
4. Jesus <u>replaces</u> my sinful past with his perfect life.
5. Jesus also relived the history of <u>Old Testament</u> Israel.
6. Even though Jesus relived Israel's history perfectly, he still accepted the <u>consequences</u> of Israel's failure.

7. In doing this, Jesus <u>became</u> the new Israel.
8. Revelation 5:10 places on the new Israel the <u>responsibilities</u> of Old Testament Israel: Christ and his church.
9. In Revelation, references to Israel cannot refer to <u>nationality</u> or ethnicity or geography.
10. References to Israel in Revelation refer to <u>spiritual</u> Israel.
11. The entire key to understanding Revelation is to see it in the light of <u>relationship</u> to Jesus Christ.

Chapter 7
1. The purpose of Revelation is to show God's people what is going to happen <u>soon</u>.
2. There is a special connection between <u>Daniel</u> and Revelation.
3. Revelation is concerned with the time of the <u>end</u>.
4. In understanding Revelation we must take into account Daniel's <u>prophecies</u> and Jesus' words concerning the last days.
5. <u>Symbolism</u> is the rule for Revelation, not literalism. It is the default mode.
6. John didn't <u>make up</u> Revelation; he wrote down what Jesus showed him.
7. Revelation was intended to be <u>understood</u> by us and those in the past.

Chapter 8
1. Revelation 10 identifies a special group of <u>people</u> who will carry a special message, and when they will do it.
2. Revelation 10 and Daniel 12 are <u>parallel</u> passages.
3. In Daniel 12 the scroll is <u>sealed</u>. In Revelation 10 the scroll is open.
4. Daniel 12 is the <u>climax</u> to a prophecy that begins in Daniel 8.
5. In Revelation 10 John is taking into account the entire <u>context</u> of the vision from Daniel 8–12.
6. Only the time prophecies of Daniel aren't explained in Daniel. They are the "<u>sealed</u>" prophecies.
7. The open scroll in Revelation 10 symbolizes the time when Daniel's <u>time</u> prophecies would be understood.
8. "There will be no more delay," means "there will be no more <u>time</u> prophecies."
9. After the time prophecies end, then the <u>mystery</u> of God will be finished.

10. The mystery of God is the <u>gospel</u> going to the whole world.
11. There will be an <u>unknown</u> period of time between the end of the time prophecies of Daniel and the second coming of Christ.
12. God's end-time special messengers are those who <u>unsealed</u> the time prophecies.
13. They bring a special <u>message</u> during the time of the end, the time when the mystery of God is being finished.
14. This special message will include:
    a. <u>Gospel</u>
    b. <u>Prophecy</u>
    c. <u>Sanctuary</u>
    d. With special <u>relevance</u> to the last days.

Chapter 9
1. Revelation 12 is a prophetic overview of <u>Christian</u> history.
2. Each time a new character is introduced in Revelation, John takes a moment to <u>describe</u> that character.
3. If what seems like a new character appears in the story but without a <u>description</u>, we have probably seen this character before under a different name or symbol.
4. It seems as though Revelation has many <u>characters</u>, but there are only a few characters represented by different names and symbols.
5. The woman of Revelation 12 represents the <u>people</u> of God in some form.
6. The red dragon is <u>Satan</u>. The male child is Jesus.
7. Michael in Revelation 12 has to be <u>Jesus</u>, and this does not mean that he is a created angel.
8. The three stages of Christian history are:
    a. Stage one: The time of <u>Jesus</u> and the apostles (Revelation 12:5, 10–12).
    b. Stage two: The time of the <u>Middle Ages</u> and beyond (Revelation 12:6, 14–16).
    c. Stage three: The time of earth's final <u>conflict</u> (Revelation 12:17).
9. The 42 <u>months</u>, 1,260 <u>days</u>, and a time, times, and half a time all refer to the same time period.
10. The day-for-a-year principle should be considered for <u>unusual</u> numbers and when the situation requires it.
11. The serpent spewing water out of his mouth is an allusion to the ser-

pent deceiving Eve in Genesis 3.

12. Satan attacks God's people through persecution and deception.
13. The children of the woman are God's end-time people.
14. Revelation 12:17 sets the stage for the final conflict of earth's history.

Chapter 10

1. Revelation 12:17 sets the stage for the final conflict of earth's history.
2. Before diving into the dragon's side of the battle, Revelation describes the new character: the beast from the sea.
3. The tenses of Greek grammar support this structure of Revelation 13.
4. The sea beast of Revelation 13 is a composite of the beasts of Daniel 7.
5. The animals in Daniel's vision were all political powers.
6. The sea beast has a background of political power, but the fact that it also blasphemes God is a strong clue that this is also a religious power.
7. The fatal wound and resurrection of the sea beast is a counterfeit of the death and resurrection of Jesus.
8. The dragon gives authority to the sea beast and seems to be setting itself up to be a counterfeit of God the Father.
9. The clues concerning the identity of the beast are piling up:
    a. played a powerful religious and political role for more than 1,000 years;
    b. entered a time of obscurity;
    c. has the potential of being resurrected into power again;
    d. has a history of persecution of other Christians;
    e. will have a rival gospel with a Christian message.
10. The land beast starts out good, but in the end it supports the dragon.
    a. It has no significant history.
    b. It points the earth toward the sea beast by forcing people to worship it.
    c. It brings fire down from heaven.
    d. It creates an image and breathes life into it.
11. The primary issue in the final conflict will be worship.
12. The mark of the beast is a parallel to the seal of God (Revelation 7 and 14).
13. The mark of the beast and seal of God are signs of loyalty to one or the other.

187

14. One of the best <u>biblical</u> explanations of 666 may lie in the story of Nebuchadnezzar's image in Daniel 3: the creation of an image, an order to worship it, and death to any who refuse.

Chapter 11
1. Revelation is a description of the final <u>conflict</u> from the side of God and his people.
2. The marks of God's end-time remnant people include:
    a. Mark 1: They keep all the <u>commandments</u>.
    b. Mark 2: The have the <u>testimony</u> of Jesus, which is the gift of prophecy.
    c. Mark 3: They are the object of worldwide <u>attention</u>.
    d. Mark 4: They are the object of economic <u>sanctions</u>.
    e. Mark 5: They are the focus of a worldwide <u>coalition</u> of opposition.
    f. Mark 6: They carry a message <u>significant</u> to the entire world.
3. "The remnant of Revelation would seem to be a worldwide, spiritual, <u>last-day</u> group drawn from every worldwide organization and government" (Jon Paulien).
4. The remnant of Revelation seems to be marked by its character and its message rather than by affiliation with any particular <u>organization</u>.
5. It seems that the last-day remnant of Revelation does not yet <u>exist</u> in its final form.

Chapter 12
1. The remnant, the <u>144,000,</u> and the great multitude that cannot be numbered are different names for the same group of people.
2. The remnant of Revelation will reflect the <u>character</u> of Jesus, including strength, authority, courage, and fearlessness.
3. "Kept themselves pure" refers to <u>loyalty</u> to God.
4. "Following the Lamb wherever he goes" refers to a continuous <u>relationship</u> with Jesus.
5. "No lie was found in their mouths" indicates the fact that God's people will be <u>authentic</u> about their true condition.
6. The double message of the cross is that because of our condition, we are <u>lost</u>, but regardless of that condition, we are acceptable to God in Jesus.
7. "They are blameless" refers to the fact that God's people are <u>becoming</u> like Jesus.

8. We can be blameless right now simply by giving Jesus permission to begin his work of <u>transforming</u> our lives.

9. The three angels' messages represent the <u>gospel</u> going to the world: evangelism.

10. The final message of God's last-day people will be grounded in the <u>gospel</u>.

11. The three major commands of Revelation 14:7 are: <u>fear</u> God, <u>give</u> him glory, and <u>worship</u> him.

12. We should pay attention to these commands because judgment has already begun during the time of the final <u>proclamation</u> of the gospel.

13. The three times of judgment are:
    a. At the <u>cross</u>
    b. Each time the cross is <u>preached</u>
    c. <u>Judgment</u> at the end.

14. This pre-Advent judgment is a call to be <u>accountable</u> to God in even the little things of life.

15. Judgment will set <u>wrongs</u> right again.

Chapter 13

1. Four ways we can fear God is by:
   a. Taking him <u>seriously</u>
   b. Being in intimate <u>relationship</u> with him
   c. <u>Obeying</u> him
   d. Avoiding <u>evil</u>

2. Three ways we can give God glory is by:
   a. Making it clear who is doing the <u>work</u> in us
   b. Living a <u>healthy</u>, vibrant life
   c. Being <u>grateful</u>

3. Revelation 14:7 is the center of the center of the center of the book of Revelation, and it strongly alludes to the first four <u>commandments</u> in Exodus.

4. The beast of Revelation 13 has a <u>counterfeit</u> of the first four commandments.

5. The fourth commandment is the <u>seal</u> of God.

6. The counterfeit fourth commandment is the <u>mark</u> of the beast.

Chapter 14

1. The key to the battle of Armageddon begins in the <u>sixth</u> plague.
2. If the prostitute is the same as Babylon, then the many waters of Revelation 17 must be the <u>Euphrates</u>.
3. The Euphrates River represents <u>peoples</u> and <u>multitudes</u> and <u>nations</u> and <u>tongues/languages</u>.
4. Long before Revelation was written, the Euphrates River was already a symbol of Babylon's <u>resources</u>.
5. When Jeremiah says that the Euphrates dries up, it means God casting <u>judgment</u> on Babylon's strength, resources, and defenses.
6. When her resources are dried up, Babylon <u>falls</u>.
7. The battle of Armageddon is all about the fall of <u>Babylon</u>.
8. Cyrus is called <u>messiah</u> because he is the one who rescues God's oppressed people by drying up the Euphrates to conquer Babylon.
9. Cyrus is a symbol of <u>Jesus</u>.
10. The kings of the East are <u>Jesus</u> and those with him rescuing his people.
11. The battle of Armageddon is not primarily a military conflict; it is a battle for the mind, a <u>spiritual</u> war.
12. Armageddon is the climax of the final conflict in which <u>spiritual</u> deception is the dragon's primary strategy.

Chapter 15

1. Revelation 17 is probably one of the <u>toughest</u> parts of the Bible to understand.
2. What John sees (vision) and what he hears (explanation) is always the <u>same</u> thing in Revelation.
3. Many waters, kings of the earth, and the scarlet beast are <u>different</u> names for the same thing.
4. All these symbols represent a <u>union</u> of civil political powers.
5. The prostitute of Revelation 17 alludes to Israel's <u>high priest</u>.
6. Babylon may well represent a worldwide confederacy of <u>religion</u>, supported by the political powers of the world.
7. In the last days, the religions and the political powers of the world will find a reason to <u>unite</u>.
8. The three confederacies of Armageddon are:
    a. <u>Political</u> confederacy
    b. <u>Religious</u> confederacy
    c. Confederacy of the <u>saints</u>

9. Babylon is the sum total of the <u>counterfeit</u> trinity.
10. At the end of time, religious authority will come to <u>dominate</u> the world once more.
11. Armageddon is primarily a <u>spiritual</u> conflict.
12. The result of the battle of Armageddon is that two <u>groups</u> emerge and no one can remain neutral.
13. Babylon meets her end through the <u>political</u> powers that supported her.
14. I choose now to love the truth, and I am willing to follow the Lamb wherever He goes. Yes or no. There's no middle ground.

Chapter 16
1. The 12 steps in the sequence of final events are:
    a. Step 1: The true <u>gospel</u> will go to the entire world.
    b. Step 2: The <u>counterfeit</u> gospel will go to the entire world.
    c. Step 3: Everyone must <u>choose</u> between the true and the counterfeit.
    d. Step 4: Babylon convinces the world with <u>miraculous</u> signs.
    e. Step 5: Babylon and the political powers <u>unite</u>.
    f. Step 6: The people of God are threatened with <u>death</u>.
    g. Step 7: Probation <u>closes</u>.
    h. Step 8: The <u>saints</u> are attacked.
    i. Step 9: God miraculously <u>intervenes</u> on behalf of the saints.
    j. Step 10: The political powers <u>destroy</u> Babylon.
    k. Step 11: The <u>political</u> powers are destroyed at the Second Coming.
    l. Step 12: God's people go to meet the Lord in the <u>air</u>.
2. Imagining the future is dangerous if we are too <u>confident</u> in our imagination.

Chapter 17
1. Signs of Jesus' return:
    a. The gospel goes out in a way <u>significant</u> to the world (Matt. 24:14).
    b. Most people will not <u>expect</u> Jesus' return when it happens (Matt. 24:38, 1 Thess. 5:1, 2).
    c. False impersonators working <u>miracles</u> will claim to be Jesus (Matt. 24:24).
    d. After the tribulation, the sun and moon will be <u>darkened</u> and the stars will fall just before Jesus arrives (Matt. 24:29, 30).

191

2. The actual Second Coming:
    a. Jesus will come in the <u>clouds</u> (Matt. 24:30).
    b. Everyone on earth will actually <u>see</u> Jesus come (Rev. 1:7).
    c. Jesus' coming will be like <u>lightning</u> flashing from the east to the west (Matt. 24:27) and no one will be unconvinced of the reality of it.
    d. Jesus will be <u>accompanied</u> by thousands and thousands of beings (Jude 14).
    e. The Second Coming will be <u>noisy</u> (1 Thess. 4:16).
    f. The Second Coming will be marked by a massive <u>resurrection</u> of the redeemed (1 Thess. 4:16).
    g. At the trumpet blast, the redeemed will be instantly <u>changed</u> physically and mentally (1 Cor. 15:51, 52).
    h. The redeemed will <u>shout</u> Isaiah 29:5 together.
    i. The Second Coming will include <u>judgment</u> (Matthew 16:27).
    j. The Second Coming will be accompanied by <u>destruction</u> (1 Thess. 5:3).
    k. The <u>redeemed</u> will be caught up to meet Jesus in the air (1 Thess. 4:17).
3. Do not concentrate on what the <u>counterfeit</u> might look like; concentrate on what the real thing will be like.